Best wi—
to you o—
stay in tou—
with your old
Pals at Iowa

Paul
(Russell &
Renata too)
Sept 2004

# Italian Literature and Thought Series

The Italian Literature and Thought Series makes available in English representative works of Italian culture. Although the series focuses on the modern and contemporary periods, it does not neglect the humanistic roots of Italian thought. The series includes monographs, anthologies, and critically updated republications of canonical works, as well as works of general interest.

# Persuasion & Rhetoric

CARLO MICHELSTAEDTER

*Translated with an introduction and commentary by*
Russell Scott Valentino,
Cinzia Sartini Blum,
and David J. Depew

Yale University Press    New Haven & London

Published with assistance from the Ernst Cassirer Publication Fund.

Designed by Sonia Shannon.
Set in Minion type by Integrated Publishing Solutions.
Printed in the United States of America by Sheridan Books.

Library of Congress Cataloging-in-Publication Data
Michelstaedter, Carlo, 1887–1910.
    [Persuasione e la rettorica. English]
    Persuasion and rhetoric / Carlo Michelstaedter ; translated with
an introduction and commentary by Russell Scott Valentino,
Cinzia Sartini Blum, and David J. Depew.
        p.   cm. — (Italian literature and thought series)
    Includes bibliographical references and index.
    ISBN 0-300-10434-0 (alk. paper)
    1. Persuasion (Rhetoric)   I. Valentino, Russell Scott, 1962–
II. Blum, Cinzia Sartini.    III. Depew, David J., 1942–   IV. Title.
V. Series.
    P301.5.P47M5313 2004
    808—dc22                                          2004043420

A catalogue record for this book is available from the
British Library.

The paper in this book meets the guidelines for permanence and
durability of the Committee on Production Guidelines for Book
Longevity of the Council on Library Resources.

10 9 8 7 6 5 4 3 2 1

# Contents

# Acknowledgments

This book was greatly facilitated by financial support from the Obermann Center for Advanced Studies at the University of Iowa, in the form of an interdisciplinary collaborative research grant, and by the good-humored encouragement of center director Jay Semel.

# Introduction

## Carlo Michelstaedter's
### *Persuasion and Rhetoric*

DAVID J. DEPEW,

RUSSELL SCOTT VALENTINO,

AND CINZIA SARTINI BLUM

Born on June 3, 1887, in Gorizia, a predominantly Catholic town of five thousand inhabitants to the northeast of Trieste, Carlo Michelstaedter was the youngest of four children in a cultured Jewish Italian family. His father, Alberto, was the Gorizia director of the Hapsburg insurance giant *Assicurazioni generali di Trieste* and president of a local literary association. His paternal great grandfather, Reggio Michelstaedter, widely known for his learning, was the rabbi of the town's Jewish minority, most of whose members, including Carlo's mother, Emma Luzzatto, and his elder sister, Elda Morpurgo, would later perish in the Holocaust.

Although neither Carlo nor his immediate family was observant, the specific challenges of "Occidental Jewry" arguably played a formative role in the young Gorizian's intellectual persona as, in Ladislao Mittner's phrase, yet another "man without a home." In this he is comparable to such contemporaries as Franz Kafka, Arthur Schnitzler, and Italo Svevo, all of whom underwent similar human and artistic experiences amid the multilingual, multiethnic ambience of late-Hapsburg central Europe.[1] Destined like other sons of the Jewish *haute bourgeoisie* for more leisured, scholarly, and artistic lives than their fathers, Carlo identified more with Italy than with Austria, in particular with Italian humanism. After graduating from the Gorizia gymnasium and after a brief period in which he considered studying mathematics at the University of Vienna, he turned south in 1905 and enrolled in the Faculty of Letters at the Institute of Higher Studies in Florence, where he remained until 1909.

His years in Florence were filled with study and intellectual growth but also with repeated failures and disillusionment. His attempts to join the editorial staffs of several publications were unsuccessful, as were his proposals for the translation of various works from German. His close friendship with the young Russian divorcee Nadia Baraden ended tragically with her suicide in 1907, and his intended engagement with a Catholic classmate, Iolanda De Blasi, met stiff opposition from his family. His childhood companion Enrico Mreule departed for Argentina, not to return in Michelstaedter's lifetime,[2] and his brother died under mysterious circumstances in New York. In the end, suffering from isolation and a depressive melancholy that would accompany him to the end of his brief life, Carlo returned to the familiar atmosphere of Gorizia in 1909 to prepare his dissertation.

The dissertation, *Persuasion and Rhetoric*, together with six critical appendices that expand and further elaborate the arguments of the main part,[3] were submitted by mail to the University of Florence on October 16, 1910. The following day Michelstaedter killed himself by firing, if a contemporary newspaper account is to be believed, more than one shot from a revolver.[4]

Although no action was apparently taken by Michelstaedter's doctoral committee, *Persuasion and Rhetoric* (without the important preface and the scholarly critical appendices) was published in 1913 by his friend Vladimiro Arangio Ruiz. It was republished by Emilio Michelstaedter, Carlo's cousin, in 1922; again, as part of Michelstaedter's *Opere*, edited by Gaetano Chiavacci, in 1958; by Maria Raschini in 1972; and finally, in a critical edition based on two manuscripts (A, in Michelstaedter's hand, and C, copied by someone else) that had been deposited by the author's family in the civic library of Gorizia, by Sergio Campailla, in 1982. Campailla's edition, which was translated with editors' notes into French in 1989 (Editions de L'éclat), forms the basis for the present translation, the first into English.

The staying power of a text by an immature author who was never personally in a position to defend his brainchild can be explained only in terms of the continued resonance his work has had for several generations downwind of the crisis of values so deeply etched in it. It is that continuing power, some of which springs from the heightened consciousness and preternatural sensitivity for cultural crisis that those living at the margins of cultures frequently exhibit, that is the main subject of this introduction.

The full title of the manuscript of Michelstaedter's dissertation was *The Concepts of Persuasion and Rhetoric in Plato and Aristotle*. This names a conventional topic of the sort that might well form the basis of a dissertation in classical philology or philosophy. Michelstaedter's professorial committee, members of a faculty of letters in the high humanist tradition, which stressed the study of modern as well as classical languages and made few forced distinctions between philosophical and literary texts, would have been well placed to judge such a submission. Among the members of the committee was, for example, the classical philologist Girolamo Vitelli. Vitelli's work is, by our standards, very wide in scope (but no wider than that of learned contemporary German philologists such as Ulrich von Wilomowitz-Moellendorff). It includes papyrological reconstructions, editions of Euripides' plays as well as of Philoponus's commentary on Aristotle's *Physics*, papers about Aeschylus, a handbook of Latin literature, a report about the difference between classical and romantic philology, and a surprisingly recurrent fascination with the work of Giordano Bruno, burned at the stake for opposing the authority of the church in matters cosmological at the dawn of the scientific revolution.

Any philologically informed work on the topic of rhetoric and persuasion in Plato and Aristotle would normally begin from the fact that Plato, reacting strongly to the sophists, condemned rhetoric—addressed speech meant to persuade an audience—as unprincipled, deceptive, and in the service of private advantage. Some of the sophists in Plato's environment, such as Gorgias, were proud of the fact that rhetoric has the power to deceive: Plato was not making the accusation up out of whole cloth. His deepest attack on rhetoric as deception, *apate*, can be found in his dialogue *Gorgias*. Later, however, Plato seems to have relented in his condemnation of rhetoric, but only because he began to invent a reformed rhetoric—hardly rhetorical at all by normal standards—that would not be subject to the objections he himself had raised. Plato's student Aristotle also approved of rhetoric, indeed regarded it as an art. But Aristotle's rhetoric, with its stress on rational argument and on the authority of the speaker as an ethical persona, was no less hostile than Plato's to sophistic rhetoric as such.

In Michelstaedter's *Persuasion and Rhetoric* we find none of these traditional issues and topics. Plato and Aristotle are analyzed extensively in only one section of the text (in Part Two, Chapter I, "A Historical Example"), and then in an oblique and parabolic fashion. The conventions of the academic genre in which Michelstaedter writes seem thereby to be subverted, and this is a tactic that he admits to employing as early as the preface: "I do not pay for entrance into any of the established categories," he writes, "or establish precedents for any new category." As Campailla puts it, "The young writer develops a personal discourse, which breaks free from the premises of scholarly exercise" (Campailla, *Persuasione* 13).

A closer look reveals that Michelstaedter writes and indeed writes seriously about the meaning of and relation between the terms "rhetoric" and "persuasion." He discusses these concepts, however, from a perspective that explicitly adopts the tradition of darkly poetic and pessimistic philosophical wisdom first manifested in the pre-Socratic philosopher-poets and in the Athenian tragedians on whom Michelstaedter extensively comments in *Persuasion and Rhetoric,* a tradition, in his opinion, subverted by the optimistic system-building absolutism of Plato and Aristotle. It is clear, if not explicit, that Plato and Aristotle stand in for the pie-in-the-sky systemizations of Croce and other neo-Hegelian idealists who dominated the contemporary Italian intellectual scene and that Michelstaedter is casting his lot with Schopenhauer, Nietzsche, Giacomo Leopardi, and others (Tolstoy, Ibsen, Sorel) who called this official wisdom into question.

What Michelstaedter means by "persuasion" is the state of consciousness and being in which an entity, any entity, is entirely at one with itself and the world, entirely present and true to itself and others. Inspection of fragments of the *Poem* of

Parmenides reveals a likely source of Michelstaedter's peculiarly extended, yet quite precise conception of persuasion. Parmenides, having contrasted the "way of being," which the wise discern, with the way of seeming, which the many are condemned to live, comments, "The one way, namely, that which is and cannot not-be, is the path of persuasion (*peithos*), for it attends truth (*aletheia*)" (Diels 2). "My life and the world I live are one and the same," claims Parmenides. Thought and thing must be identical, for only thought that grasps an existent object counts as such, and the act of asserting ("it is") must affirm the existent as existing on pain of not being an act of asserting at all. Negative existentials are impossible. From this Parmenides infers that the world as it is must be one, indivisible, and without negativity (which permits us to say "this is not that"). All thought is inherently referential. Hence anything that is referred to must exist. This means that any degree of negativity—*a* is not-*b*—is a referential misfire. All things that exist must be one completely homogeneous substance, and it is this ontological state that Michelstaedter appears to use as a symbol, or perhaps more than a symbol, for the psychological state of being fully persuaded: the persuaded, authentic, just person must will one thing alone. It is likely that this Hellenocentric approach leads him to the claim that the Greek way of establishing idealism is far superior to its modern form.

What, by contrast, Michelstaedter means by "rhetoric" is the endless series of deceptions by which we try to convince ourselves and each other that we are persuaded: satisfied, fulfilled, "happy." By treating the two concepts in this way, the normal relation between persuasion and rhetoric is broken. As Daniela Bini puts it, "The rhetorician speaks in order to persuade and convince through the force of his arguments.

*Retorica* and *persuasione,* thus, go hand in hand. Not for Michelstaedter, however, who considered them opposites" (*Carlo Michelstaedter* 5). The turn away from this truth, exemplified by the systematizing rhetoric of Plato and Aristotle that furnishes the ostensible material for his thesis, has, according to Michelstaedter, recurred again and again throughout the history of European thought. For Michelstaedter, then, no entity can be fully persuaded, for existence is *eX-sistence,* standing out in a temporally distended space between past and future entirely characterized by desire, striving, yearning for the very presence, satiety, that it never attains on condition of not being what it is. As soon as an entity obtains what it desires, that which was heretofore absent from its wanting state, yet another object of desire presents itself, and then others ad infinitum. This is the image strikingly developed in Michelstaedter's opening discussion of a weight whose yearning for each successive point below it in infinite descent precludes the possibility of persuasion.

In this connection, Michelstaedter places himself in the voluntarist tradition of Schopenhauer, Hegel's great opponent in the early nineteenth century, who regarded life as a disease, permanent lack, endless pain, crucifixion on a cross of ceaseless desires and illusory representations of their fulfillment. The connection to Schopenhauer explains Michelstaedter's invocations of the Buddha. Michelstaedter's Buddha, like that of Schopenhauer, preaches that the extinction of desire is the only possible wisdom for human beings. In this respect, Michelstaedter is closer to Schopenhauer and to Leopardi, whose attitudes and tones he clearly imitated, than he is to Nietzsche. Nietzsche was no less voluntaristic, and no less an adept of dark wisdom, than Schopenhauer. But Nietzsche, especially in the character of Zarathustra, put a decidedly more upbeat

stress on how the tragic wisdom of the ancients could facilitate
a wholesale personal and cultural transformation of values toward heroic resistance than does Michelstaedter.

The divergence from Neitzsche also throws light on Michelstaedter's divergence from noted voluntarists in his general vicinity. The Italian futurists, in particular F. T. Marinetti,
are worth mentioning in this connection. Michelstaedter and
Marinetti exemplify two different yet equally extreme outcomes
of the spiritual malaise that affected, in the words of Giuseppe
Antonio Borgese, the "unhappy intellectual and provincial
bourgeoisie, twisted by their 'all-or-nothing' upbringing, spoiled
by their taste for definitive ascensions" (99). In response to the
modern crisis of absolutes, both authors rejected rationalist
and idealist systems of values without relinquishing the will to
autonomous self-definition at the origin of such systems. But
for Michelstaedter absolute control could be reached only by
means of the Schopenhauerean strategy of suppressing or
eliminating desire for life. Marinetti, by contrast, attacked the
suicidal pessimism of Schopenhauer, "the bitter philosopher
who so often threatens with the seductive revolver of his philosophy to destroy our profound nausea for *Amore* with a cap-
ital *A*."[5] Proclaiming a new, "artificial" optimism, Marinetti
assimilated the chaotic forces of modernity—in Michelstaedter's terms, the ultimate realm of rhetoric—as the means to an
aggressive program of individual and national regeneration.
His futurist *modernolatria* is a far cry from Michelstaedter's
apology for the "untimely wisdom" of a timeless truth.

Still, none of this is to deny that when he speaks of *attualità*, 'presentness,' 'actuality,' Michelstaedter explicitly adopts
Nietzsche's notion of "untimely wisdom" (*unzeitgemässige Re-
flectionen*), that is, of saying things, as his first epigraph from
Sophocles emphasizes, that are against the spirit of the time.

For Nietzsche, and Michelstaedter after him, German *Historismus* is a particular object of untimely attack. *Historismus,* in Nietzsche's view, puts detailed scholarship in the service of a progressive social mythology that, by its very weightiness, kills the spirit of life, will, and innovation. In opposing *Historismus,* Michelstaedter assumes that there is a *philosophia perennis,* a truth that wise people have discovered again and again but that is necessarily lost again and again because most people, adrift in what Montaigne and Pascal call "distraction" and what Heidegger, in *Being and Time,* was to call "the they" (*das Mann*), cannot bear the truth and will do anything to avoid it. They invent *kallopismata orfnes,* 'ornaments of the darkness,' the rhetorical commonplaces that allow them to live without understanding. And in this, Michelstaedter emphasizes repeatedly, they are aided by the "god" of *philopsychia,* 'pleasure,' 'attachment to life,' or, as he translates the term in a footnote, *viltà,* 'cowardice.'

In his preface Michelstaedter lists Parmenides, Empedocles, Socrates, the great Greek tragedians Aeschylus and Sophocles, the lyric poet Simonides, the Jewish but Hellenizing author of Ecclesiastes, Christ, and subsequently the humanist Petrarch, then Leopardi, Ibsen, and Beethoven (to whose music Michelstaedter was deeply attached). There is a message in this admittedly incomplete list: people who, in philosophy and literature courses, are usually said to be representative of the philosophia perennis, the great professional philosophers such as Plato, Aristotle, and Aquinas, not to speak of Hegel, Croce, and Gentile, are explicitly said by Michelstaedter *not* to have this insight. Their optimistic, official, intellectualist philosophy of illusory fulfillment is an ideological product of the desire to cover up the basic truth. In the great battle between intellectualists and voluntarists, they are the intellectualists, who tell us that behind life's curtain lies the possibility of totally satisfactory presence. The philosophia perennis advocated by Michelstaedter invokes a voluntarist pantheon.

This brings us to a second, perhaps more impressive and original, way in which Michelstaedter emulates Nietzsche. As a Greek scholar of considerable skill, Michelstaedter was well prepared to follow Nietzsche's philological lead in looking for the true Greek wisdom not in Academic, Peripatetic, Stoic, or Epicurean traditions but in the often paradoxical and always fragmentary pre-Socratics—Parmenides, Heraclitus, Empedocles, and the tragedians, especially Sophocles and Aeschylus. In his early work *The Birth of Tragedy out of the Spirit of Music,* Nietzsche, who was a professional Greek scholar, began by quoting a piece of this old dark wisdom in which a wise man, intervening in the conventional debate about how to rank the best things in life, says, "The best thing is not to have been born at all; the second best to die young." Nietzsche would continue this vein in his *Philosophy in the Tragic Age of the Greeks.* What is most original about Michelstaedter's work is that he was virtually the first person to see that the ancient language of rhetoric, rather than its rival, the Platonic language of philosophy, is the best medium in which both to restore the meaning of true, dark Greek wisdom and to commend it again. By taking this surprising approach, Michelstaedter anticipates a good deal of subsequent and contemporary scholarship concerning the origins of Greek rhetoric in the *Logos* tradition that was eventually undermined by Platonic philosophy. "The *Logos* always holds," says Heraclitus, "but humans always prove unable to understand it" (Diels 1).

In his highly original, if unsystematic, interpretation of the pre-Socratic fragments, Michelstaedter anticipates in striking ways the work of Martin Heidegger. In *Being and Time*

(1926), Heidegger provided a phenomenology of lived experience that makes the awareness of death central in opening the temporal structure of human life (*Dasein*) as a series of desires. Michelstaedter's distinction between "persuasion" and "rhetoric" is close to Heidegger's distinction between authenticity and the inauthentic chatter of *das Mann*. Like Michelstaedter, moreover, Heidegger eventually saw that he was in a position to appreciate Heraclitus's dialectical view that each thing, being mortal, is interpenetrated with its opposite. "The same thing," says Heraclitus, "is both living and dead" (Diels 126). That is why for Heraclitus "all things flow" like a river into which one cannot step twice. The awareness and acceptance of that dark opposite, and the refusal to merely "reflect" the various and sundry kallopismata with which rhetoric covers it, are of fundamental concern for Michelstaedter. Long after he had intimated, in *Persuasion and Rhetoric,* that Parmenides and Heraclitus were proclaiming the same Logos and were not the opposites that Aristotle, Hegel, and other official philosophers considered them to be (the first supposedly being a radical "monist," the second a radical "pluralist"), Heidegger would assert the very same thing. This convergence is not surprising. It was only after his deep encounter with Nietzsche that Heidegger came to grasp the dark Logos of the pre-Socratics.

Few of Michelstaedter's assertions are in themselves altogether new. On the contrary, he is highly intertextual. The reader, if he or she is to gain wisdom—to be persuaded, in Michelstaedter's vocabulary—is expected to work through citations and allusions rather than merely recognize where they come from. In this allusive manner, the book is reminiscent of Hegel's *Phenomenology of Spirit,* a work that seeks to lead the reader through the gallery of "pictures" of the human condition that must successively be undergone if true illumination is to occur. Thus, when Michelstaedter claims, in Part One, Chapter II, that "nothing is for itself but with respect to consciousness," he reiterates a key proposition of Hegel's *Phenomenology*. The opening phrase of Part One, moreover, echoes Hegel's concept of the "Philosopher": "If we want to be nasty, we can say that the Philosopher is discontented because he does not *know* what he wants. But if we want to be just, we must say that he is discontented because he does not know what he *wants*. He has desires, like everyone. But the satisfaction of his desires does not satisfy him, as Philosopher, as long as he does not understand them, that is, as long as he does not fit them into the coherent *whole* of his discourse that reveals his existence" (Kojève 86). Michelstaedter's treatment, however, moves beyond the philosopher per se, suggesting in the subsequent oblique comparison of himself to a gluttonous chlorine molecule that the absence with which he is concerned is a broadly human rather than a strictly philosophical dilemma.

In the end, Michelstaedter's wisdom is the very opposite of Hegel's, as he makes explicit in the closing chapters. He is, as we have noted, radically voluntaristic rather than intellectualistic in his mode of thinking: the human condition is not oriented toward theoretical appreciation, as it is for Hegel and Hegel's master, Aristotle, but is defined instead by desire and its frustration, as Schopenhauer had insisted. All the figures of whom Michelstaedter approves are voluntarists in this sense or are interpreted by him in this way.

Nor does Michelstaedter think, as Hegel did, that the truth about the human condition becomes much clearer as modernity proceeds. On the contrary, clear thinking—again, conviction, persuasion—becomes ever more compromised by rhetoric as modernity sets in. This too is clear at the end of the text, where Michelstaedter ridicules the pretensions of the self-satisfied bourgeois in ways that recall, and may well depend on, Leopardi, Kierkegaard, Nietzsche, Tolstoy,[6] and, most explicitly, Ibsen. Accordingly, all the textual materials on which Michelstaedter meditates—even the most up to date—are placed into a frame that privileges the pre-Socratic Greek philosophers and dramatists (and a few brave souls thereafter) as offering an unblinkered peek at the fundamental reality of the human condition. It is these figures who are given defining control over the key term "persuasion," and, by extension, "rhetoric."

One of the first things Michelstaedter shows is that the use of the term *pithenon* meant to the pre-Socratics total conviction. This fact provides a clue to understanding why he at least pretends that he has written a dissertation in classical Greek philology. In some ways he has. In this respect, Michelstaedter once more resembles Nietzsche, a classical philologist who explicitly spurned the fundamental project of German idealism: to unify the Greco-Roman with the Judeo-Christian inheritance and to define modernity as lying at the confluence of both. In contrast to Kierkegaard, who chose the Judeo-Christian side, Michelstaedter instead opted, like Nietzsche, for the hard wisdom of the early Greeks. In this respect he was perhaps at his most innovative, anticipating the path toward the pre-Socrates that Heidegger would later tread. This, we believe, explains one of the fundamental oddities of Michelstaedter's text: when he wants throughout the manuscript to state his own conclusions, he translates them into Greek, as if he were offering a serious exhibition to his readers both of his skill in Greek composition and of the crystalline truth at the center of his thought. The most succinct example of this occurs in the portion of Part One, Chapter III that is concerned with the true meaning of giving, which Michelstaedter defines by means of an exclamation point following the Greek word:

"*Giving is not for the sake of having given but for giving* (δοναι!)."
The truth is contained in the word; the word is the truth. A
more telling illustration of the unity of philosophy and philology that underlies Michelstaedter's approach, and of the simultaneity of word, truth, and action envisioned in his project, is impossible to imagine.

Although many significant links can be traced between
Michelstaedter and German thinkers, it is also significant that
no German author makes the famous list in the preface. Indeed Michelstaedter explicitly warns against the pernicious effect of German writers in a bibliography found among the papers on his desk ("these are contagious, just by looking at
them"). We might surmise that their contagious influence has
to do with the insidious rhetoric of knowledge. In fact, he rec-
ommends playing or listening to Beethoven's music—the un-
tainted voice of persuasion—and condemns reading as an
unnatural activity: "Eyes are not made to read books. But if
you want at any cost to lower them to this service, read: Parmenides, Heraclitus, Empedocles, Simonides, Socrates (in the
first Platonic dialogues), Aeschylus and Sophocles, Ecclesiastes, the Gospels according to Matthew, Mark and Luke, Lucretius . . . the *Triumphs* of Petrarch, and Leopardi's *Canti, The
Adventures of Pinocchio* by Collodi, Ibsen's dramas."[7]

Among the modern authors in this bibliography, Giacomo Leopardi had the clearest and most profound impact on
*Persuasion and Rhetoric*.[8] Commonly regarded as the greatest
Italian poet since Petrarch and one of the most erudite men of
his time, Leopardi professed an overtly materialistic gospel of
despair, which was untimely in an age characterized by a political and religious *rappel à l'ordre* as well as, in the most liberal
thinkers, by faith in the progress and perfectibility of humanity. Notwithstanding his classical tastes, Leopardi revealed af-

finities with romanticism in his emphasis on the poetic imagination and in his tragic vision of life, which is consonant with the pessimistic side of the movement—an undercurrent of disenchantment, unfulfilled longing, and melancholy. He gave philosophic expression to this *Weltschmerz* in a series of dialogue-essays, the *Moral Tales* (1827). In these satirical prose pieces, long before Nietzsche proclaimed the "death" of God, Leopardi addressed epistemological and moral issues that still define the modern crisis of values. Michelstaedter's central argument resonates with the most fundamental and pervasive element of Leopardi's moral philosophy, the "Theory of Pleasure," which is based on two convictions: "that we have been made with such an intense longing for happiness, and loathing for its opposite, that life itself and this longing are virtually one and the same thing; and that since we yearn for the infinite, and therefore our yearning for happiness is infinite, we can never be satisfied. Our lives therefore by their very nature are 'a violent state of being'" (Creagh 25).

*Persuasion and Rhetoric* echoes other important themes of Leopardi's thought: the critique of both contemporary scholarship and mass culture as synonymous with ignorance; the attack on the optimistic ideology of progress and on the overall cowardice of mankind; and the disillusioned defense of his own grievous philosophy as the sole courageous choice for the honest man. One might add to this list Leopardi's welcoming of death in the epilogue of the volume—the tale titled "Tristan and a Friend" (written in 1832 and included in the 1834 edition), which can be viewed as a reaction to the indifference and hostility that the 1827 edition had encountered. Note, however, that this despairing epilogue does not conclusively negate the "ingrained and ineradicable love of life" (Creagh 29) that runs through much of Leopardi's work, as he contin-

ued to celebrate magnanimous feelings and passions inspired
by values such as poetry, justice, virtue, and love, which give
purpose and meaning to life. Michelstaedter, by contrast,
brings the dark wisdom of philosophia perennis to its extreme
conclusion: he radically embraces the "frigid truth" that Leopardi resists despite his own wisdom. The sole remaining value
in Michelstaedter's moral philosophy is the honesty of persuasion, which entails a rejection of desire in its self-deceptive
wiles as well as in its exploitative (hence violent) relation to
nature and to others.

The *Moral Tales* may also be viewed as a model for the
stylistic variety of *Persuasion and Rhetoric*. Like Leopardi's dialogues, Michelstaedter's text interweaves different styles and
tones, from the lyrical to the pedantic, from the biblically
solemn to the parodically flippant. The work's first paragraph
sets the tone for the entire text by mixing the high register
(*genus grave*) of the quotation from Greek tragedy with the
low register of the colloquial, pleonastic opening (*"Io lo so che
parlo perché parlo,"* 'I know I am talking because I'm talking')
and of a quotation that sounds like a popular saying: "*è pur
necessario che se uno ha addentato una perfida sorba la risputi,*"
'if you bite into a crabapple, you've got to spit it out.'

Beyond such mixing of registers, the most remarkable
feature of Michelstaedter's style is its complexity. Whereas Leopardi's prose is difficult in a classically harmonious way, Michelstaedter's writing is expressionistically "dissonant." True to the
content of his work, Michelstaedter disavows any intention of
"persuading" or "diverting" his readers, as well as any claim to
originality, "philosophical dignity," or "artistic concreteness."
An ironic interpretation of such a paradoxical statement of
(lack of) purpose is possible: we can read it as a rhetorical
strategy (*acutum dicendi genus*) intended to produce an effect

of estrangement, which makes the reader step outside established patterns of thought (the *vie*, 'ways' or 'paths,' of which Michelstaedter writes at numerous points). This defamiliarizing effect, which can plausibly be ascribed to Heraclitus or Parmenides as no less intentional, is instrumental to the goal of persuasion as Michelstaedter conceives it. The quest for persuasion requires, as also for the Greek authors he prefers, a break with the normal world, the world Parmenides calls "the way of seeming."[9] To the same effect may be also attributed the obscurity produced throughout the text by complex sentence structures, especially by the frequent use of anastrophe (inversion), ellipsis, and anacoluthon (syntactical inconsistency or incoherence within a sentence). Now, a certain level of *obscuritas* is appropriate for the genus grave as it calls attention to the importance of the subject matter. Moreover, obscurity is the truth against which, according to Michelstaedter, we attempt to create protective and deceptive screens of light or at least ornament (kallopisma).

In view of the author's attachment to poetic and paradoxical thinkers, as well as his refusal in writing his dissertation to obey the conventions of academic prose, and, not least, the agitated state of someone who, in the very text he was writing, appears to have been working through the rationale for his own suicide, it is not surprising that his style would pose great difficulties for readers. Campailla notes that from an editor's standpoint Michelstaedter's punctuation is a "veritable *via crucis*" (*Persuasione* 29). His sentences are filled with dashes, subordinate clauses, and insufficiently identified antecedents. In translating the text, we have tried to cope with this difficulty by finding a mean between the literalness that Michelstaedter's text deserves and the responsibility to make his meaning at least as plain to English readers as it might be to Italian. The same end is served by the brief introductory statements for each section of Michelstaedter's text, and our endnote commentary is intended to provide references to some of the vast intertextual web in which Michelstaedter's book is woven.

Finally, a remark about the system of notation is in order. Michelstaedter is inconsistent in his references, sometimes paraphrasing passages represented as citations and often leaving quoted material unreferenced or only partially referenced. In the case of un- or partially referenced sources in the text, for example, the notation "(St. Luke)," we have left Michelstaedter's original notation intact and specified the appropriate passage in an endnote. Where incomplete or incorrect references are found in Michelstaedter's footnotes, we have bracketed the correct reference immediately following with the indication "Translators' note."

For the sake of readability, we have rendered Michelstaedter's numerous non-Italian expressions using appositives in single quotation marks for short words and phrases and rendering longer passages in block text immediately following. Where necessary we have likewise provided several of Michelstaedter's more idiomatic Italian expressions in the text, giving our translations of them immediately thereafter. Michelstaedter's use of the Italian "*persona*" hovers between the modern sense of "person" and the ancient designation of a "speaking role." To preserve this ambiguity, we have left *persona* (italicized) throughout the text.

All footnotes are Michelstaedter's own. The explanatory headnotes preceding each major section are intended as general indicators rather than exhaustive commentary, because the latter is work that lies outside the boundaries of the present edition.

# Notes

1. Mittner (1160–61) used the phrase ("*uomo senza casa*") to describe Kafka and Rilke. On Michelstaedter and central European Jewry, see Altieri; Campailla, "Ebraismo e letteratura"; Furlan 64–91; Pieri, *La differenza ebraica;* and Principe. For critical treatments of Michelstaedter's work in English, see Bini, *Carlo Michelstaedter;* and Harrison, *1910.*

2. This event and the fictionally constructed persona of Mreule are the subjects of Magris's 1991 novella *Un altro mare* (A Different Sea), in which Michelstaedter's ideas figure fundamentally.

3. The issue of whether the appendices constitute a part of the work is discussed in detail by Campailla, *Persuasione* 30–31.

4. "Tentato suicidio," *Gazzettino popolare,* October 18, 1910, reprinted in Gallarotti, *Il Fondo* 12.

5. Marinetti, "Multiplied Man and the Reign of the Machine," *Let's Murder the Moonshine* 100–101.

6. Although, like Nietzsche's, Tolstoy's name makes no direct appearance in *Persuasion and Rhetoric,* Michelstaedter's interest in and admiration for the man he called "the poet and apostle of the people" is evident in other writings. His September 18, 1908, article published in the *Corriere Friulano,* titled simply "Tolstoi," is devoted to the celebration of Tolstoy's eightieth birthday. In it we find many of the key phrases attributed to the persuaded or authentic individual sketched in Part One, Chapter III: "*una più vasta visione,*" 'a greater vision,' "*uniformità fra pensiero e vita,*" 'consistency of thought with life,' "*un'intuizione più vasta e più perfetta,*" 'a vaster and more perfect intuition'; he is someone who confronts "*questa società delle menzogne e le [grida] in faccia: verità! verità!*" 'this society of lies and shouts in its face: truth! truth!'

7. This page, titled "Bibliography, or God loves the illiterate," is quoted in Bini, *Carlo Michelstaedter* 159–60.

8. Several critics have noted Leopardi's influence on Michelstaedter. See, e.g., Bini 46–57 and passim.

9. A similar point about Michelstaedter's style is made by Harrison, in his *1910,* when he links Michelstaedter with other expressionist contemporaries such as Schoenberg, Kokoschka, and Trakl who, in the words of Harrison's title, "emancipate dissonance."

# Persuasion and Rhetoric

μανθάνω δ᾽ ὁθούνεκα
ἔξωρα πράσσω κοὐκ ἐμοὶ προσεικότα.

*I know my behavior is unseemly*
*and becomes me ill*[1]

# Preface

TRANSLATORS' NOTE: *The central point of the preface is to declare explicitly what is intimated by the epigraph on the title page: that Michelstaedter will not be saying what he is expected to say. He will not be writing a business-as-usual tesi di laurea, or doctoral dissertation. He will instead be repeating the spurned but perennial wisdom that he ascribes to Parmenides, Heraclitus, Empedocles, Aeschylus, Sophocles, Simonides, Socrates, the Hellenizing author of Ecclesiastes, Jesus, Petrarch, Leopardi, Ibsen, and Beethoven—each of whom becomes either an implicit or explicit object of meditation in successive chapters. What Michelstaedter will be spurning instead are the official philosophical, ecclesiastical, and literary norms that cover up the truth proclaimed fruitlessly by wise men. From the start he calls discourse that conforms to these ideological norms "rhetoric." If he brings himself to speak the negative truth at all, albeit inelegantly, it is, he says, because rhetoric, perhaps in the persons of his professorial audience, "compels him" to say something on this occasion. The pose of speaking under compulsion is, of course, also an old rhetorical formula.*

I know I am talking because I'm talking, but I also know I shall not persuade anyone, and this is dishonesty; but rhetoric ἀναγκάζει με ταῦτα δρᾶν βίᾳ, 'forcibly compels me to do things'; in other words, "if you bite into a crabapple, you've got to spit it out."[2]

Yet insofar as everything I am saying has been said many times before and with great force, it seems impossible that the world has continued each time such words have rung out.

Parmenides, Heraclitus, and Empedocles told it to the Greeks, but Aristotle treated them as untutored naturalists; Socrates said it, but they constructed four systems on him.[3] Ecclesiastes said it, but they dealt with it as a sacred book that could not therefore contradict biblical optimism; Christ said it, but they built the church upon it. Aeschylus and Sophocles and Simonides said it, and Petrarch proclaimed it triumphantly to the Italians,[4] while Leopardi repeated it with pain. But men were pleased by their pretty verses and made of them literary types. If in our time the creatures of Ibsen bring it to life in every scene, men "amuse themselves" by hearing those "exceptional" stories among all the others, and the critics speak of "symbolism"; and if Beethoven sings it so as to move the heart, then everyone turns such emotion to his own ends, making it, in the end, a question of counterpoint.

If I now repeat it insofar as I am able, because I do so in a manner to amuse no one—without philosophical dignity or artistic concreteness, but rather as a poor pedestrian measuring the terrain with his steps—if I do not pay for entrance in any of the established categories or establish precedent for some new category, even in the best of cases, I will have created . . . a doctoral thesis.

# I
# On Persuasion

# I
# Persuasion

TRANSLATORS' NOTE: *The point of this short but important chapter is to illustrate Michelstaedter's key concept of persuasion (persuasione), by which the author means to translate and amplify the Greek word* pithenon, *in the sense of complete conviction.*

*He begins by claiming that all beings, inanimate as well as animate, are defined by what they lack. A weight, for example, always seeks to fall. If having been let free it comes to rest, it is no longer a weight. "Its life is its want of life." The general implication is that, as centers of desires, nothing (and in particular nobody) can be entirely satisfied and remain what it actually is. Michelstaedter infers from this that anything that exists is also future-oriented, as he illustrates in the story about climbing to the top of a mountain. Every entity, he claims, indeed every person, is both alone and lonely, for, as long as we remain individuals, by definition we are separate centers of insatiable desire.*

*When Michelstaedter puts this point by maintaining that "the weight can never be persuaded," he implicitly defines persuasion as a hypothetical, counterfactual state in which an entity is at one with itself and its environment. Only those beings, we are given to under-*

*stand, who will the suspension of their own will can ever approach such a state. The theme is Schopenhauerian. But the sources on which Michelstaedter relies are classical. For Parmenides, the majority of people who live immersed in the Way of Seeming, and who accordingly take what is transitory and contradictory as reliable Being itself, are in a state of self-deception and illusion. They can never be "persuaded," Parmenides says, for only the Way of Being, which recognizes that there is nothing stable in experience, is "the path of persuasion (*peithos*). For it alone attends to truth (aletheia)" (Diels 2). It is in this sense that Michelstaedter uses the term persuasion throughout his work.*

Αἰθέριον μὲν γάρ σφε μένος πόντονδε διώκει,
πόντος δ᾽ ἐς χθονὸς οὖδας ἀπέπτυσε, γαῖα δ᾽ ἐς αὐγὰς
ἠελίου ἀκάμαντος, ὁ δ᾽ αἰθέρος ἔμβαλε δίναις
ἄλλος δ᾽ ἐξ ἄλλου δέχεται, στυγέουσι δὲ πάντες.

*Because the power of the ether smothers them in the
sea, / the sea spits them out on the land, the land towards
the fierce heat / of the indefatigable sun, which burns
them in the vortices of the ether; / one receives them
from the other, and all detest them.*

—Empedocles[5]

I know I want and do not have what I want. A weight hangs suspended from a hook; being suspended, it suffers because it cannot fall: it cannot get off the hook, for insofar as it is weight it suspends, and as long as it suspends it depends.

We want to satisfy it: we free it from its dependence, letting it go so that it might satisfy its hunger for what lies below, and it falls independently for as long as it is content to fall. But at none of the points attained is it content to stop; it still wants to fall, for the next point below continually overtakes in lowness that which the weight has just attained. Nor will any future point be such as to render it content, being necessary to the weight's life insofar, ὄφρα ἂν μένῃ αὐτόν,[6] as it awaits below; but every time a point is made present, it will be emptied of all attraction, no longer being below; thus does it *want at every point the points below it,* and those attract it more and more. It is always drawn by an equal hunger for what is lower, and the will to fall remains infinite with it always.

If at some point its will were finished and it could *possess* in one point the infinite descent of the infinite future, at that point it would no longer be what it is—*a weight.*

Its life is this want of life. If it no longer wanted but were finished, perfect, if it possessed its own self, it would have ended its existence. At that point, as its own impediment to possessing life, the weight would not depend on what is external as much as on its own self, in that it is not given the means to be satisfied. The weight can never be persuaded.

Nor is any life ever satisfied to live in any present, for insofar as it is life it continues, and it continues into the future to the degree that it lacks life. If it were to possess itself completely here and now and be in want of nothing—if it awaited nothing in the future—it would not continue: it would cease to be life.

So many things attract us in the future, but in vain do we want to possess them in the present.

I climb to a mountaintop:[7] its height calls me, I want to have it, and I ascend and dominate it. But how can I possess the mountain? I am truly high above the plain and sea, and I see the wide horizon from the mountain. But none of that is mine:

What I see is not within me, nor does seeing more ever mean, "I have seen": the sight, I don't possess it. The sea shines bright in the distance—that will be mine in a different manner. I shall descend to the coast. I'll hear its voice, sail along its back and . . . be content. But now on the sea, "the ear cannot be filled with hearing,"[8] the boat rides ever new waves, and "an equal thirst takes hold of me." I may plunge into it, feel a wave across my body, but where I am the sea is not. If I want to go where the water is and have it, the waves make way before the swimming man. I may drink in the saltiness, exult like a porpoise, drown myself, but I still won't possess the sea: I am alone and distinct in its midst.

Nor can a man seeking refuge in the *persona* he loves satisfy his hunger: neither kisses nor embraces nor any other demonstrations invented by love can interpenetrate one with the other: they will always be two, each alone and distinct. Men lament this solitude, but if they find it lamentable it is because being with themselves they feel alone: they feel themselves to be with no one, in want of everything.

He who is for himself (μένει) has no need of what would be for him (μένοι αὐτόν) in a future time but instead possesses all within himself.

"Has been," "shall be," and "was" will take place no
    more,
But "is" only in the present, and "now" and
    "today,"
And only the whole of eternity assembled.*[9]

---

*And Parmenides: οὔ ποτ᾽ ἔην οὐδ᾽ ἔσται, ἐπεὶ νῦν ἔστιν ὁμοῦ πᾶν, ἓν ξυνεχές, 'neither was it once nor will it be, since it is in the present, all together, one, indivisible.' [Mullach 61–62; cf. Diels 8:5–6.—Translators' note.]

But man wants from other things in a future time what he lacks in himself: *the possession of his own self,* and as he wants and is busied so with the future *he escapes himself in every present.* Thus does he move differently from the things different from him, as he is different from his own self, continuing in time. What he wants is given within him, and wanting life he distances himself from himself: he *does not know what he wants.* His end is not his end, nor does he know why he does what he does: his activity is *being passive,* for he *does not have himself* as long as an irreducible, obscure hunger for life lives within him. *Persuasion lives not in him who does not live from his own self,* who is son and father, slave and master of what lies around him, of what came before, of what must come after— a *thing among things.*

Hence is each alone and distinct among others, for his voice is not his voice, and he neither knows it nor can communicate it to others. "Words exhaust themselves" (Ecclesiastes).[10] Each pivots on his own fulcrum, which is not his own, and he cannot give to others bread he does not have himself.

*He who does not have persuasion cannot communicate it* (μήτι δύναται τυφλὸς τυφλὸν ὁδηγεῖν, 'Surely a blind man cannot lead the blind') (St. Luke).[11]

Persuaded is *he who has his life within himself,* a soul naked amongst the islands of the blessed (ἡ γυμνὴ ψυχὴ ἐν τοῖς τῶν μακάρων νήσοις) (Gorgias).[12]

But men look for τήν ψυχὴν, 'life,' and lose τὴν ψυχήν, 'life' (St. Matthew).[13]

# II

# The Illusion of Persuasion

TRANSLATORS' NOTE: *This chapter exhibits the conse-quences of the main claim of Part One, Chapter I: that the existence of all things lies in striving; that striving is the essence of existence. From this beginning point, Michelstaedter implies that all things possess philopsychia, the love of one's own sweet (physical) existence. This is a key concept in the rest of the section and one of the major motifs of the entire work. Such love implies that each of us has a de-sire, a conatus, for something that defines us, which is the focal point of all our "hunger, as if that thing could provide all [our] life." This focal concentration is an index of the state of being "persuaded," in the sense of being totally identified with. Persuasion is, as Kierke-gaard says, "to will one thing."*

*It would seem from this claim that it is well-nigh impossible for persons who are dominated by philopsychia ever fully to be per-suaded; rather, they are distracted, and so at the mercy of rhetoric. In this, they differ from animals and plants, which are always iden-tical with their desires, always focused on the specific object that de-*

*fines their striving, hence always inadequately persuaded. This raises a question: How can humans, who always live, as Heidegger says, ex-statically, standing out from themselves, toward a future, ever be persuaded? That is the central question of the treatise. An answer is sketched at the end of the chapter: by ability to bear pain, which counteracts the attachment to pleasure that defines philopsychia.*

*At this point in the text, Michelstaedter's reflection is focused on physical things and their tendencies; only in Part Two does Michelstaedter turn to the human scene as a site of reflection. He is slowly working his way from things to persons and from persons to particular forms of culture, as in Hegel's* Phenomenology. *Even here, however, Michelstaedter is using the categories of life to model physical and chemical processes. He maintains that everything that exists is the product of striving, desire, conatus. As a result, he is something of a panpsychist, at least rhetorically, as is clear in his references to the "striving" of chlorine and hydrogen to come to "life" in the form of hydrogen chloride: the concept of life is not restricted to living things but is extended to inanimate objects and processes. Michelstaedter's consistently voluntaristic perspective shows itself in the form of an apparent panpsychism—the claim that there are stirrings of consciousness in all things—and indicates the wide ambiance of vitalism and* Lebensphilosophie *that were philosophically in the ascendant during his formative years, and these, in turn, are used to code for the primacy of will over intellect in a variety of thinkers.*

*In this connection, Michelstaedter's assimilation of chemical bonding to* Lebensphilosophie *runs by way of a philological identification based on the term "valency." The valency of one chemical kind measures its affinity for another kind. The term "valency" derives from the Latin for choice. Hence the conflation, and also the in-*

*ference that the chemical kinds must have some sort of conscious-
ness, based on the notion that consciousness requires will. The same
set of tropes is at work as far back as Goethe's* Elective Affinities.

οἱ δὲ φορεῦνται
κωφοὶ ὁμῶς τυφλοί τε, τεθηπότες, ἄκριτα φῦλα,
οἷς τὸ πέλειν τε καὶ οὐκ εἶναι ταὐτὸν νενόμισται
κ᾿ οὐ ταὐτόν.

*They drag themselves, mute and blind, stupefied, a confused
multitude for whom being or not being has the same value and
does not have the same value.*

—Parmenides[14]

E ach thing that lives persuades itself that this continuous
deficiency, by which every living thing dies in continuing each instant, is life.

i

In order to possess itself, to reach actual being, it flows in time:
and *time* is infinite, for were it to succeed in possessing itself,
in consisting, it would cease to be will for life (ἄπειρον οὗ ἀεί
τι ἔξω, 'an infinity beyond which there is always something');
likewise *space* is infinite, for there is nothing that is not will for
life (ἄπειρον οὗ οὐδὲν ἔξω, 'an infinity beyond the bounds of
which lies nothing'). *Life would be* if time did not constantly

distance its being into the next instant. Life would be *one, immobile, formless* if it could consist in *one* point. The necessity of flight in time implies the necessity of the dilation of space: *perpetual mutation,* from which comes *the infinite variety of things:* ἡ φιλοψυχία παντοία γίγνεται πρὸς τὸν βίον, 'the yearning to live assumes every form reaching for life.' Because at no point is the will satisfied, each thing destroys itself in coming into being and in passing away: πάντα ῥεῖ, 'everything flows,'[15] so that it transforms itself without respite in varied desiring. And without end, without change, the indifferent transfiguration of things remains in every time whole and never completed: τόδε δὴ βίοτον καλέουσι, 'this they call life.'[16]

But who καλεῖ, 'calls'? Who says life? Who has consciousness?

If life were to secure itself in a haven, content in itself, and if it consisted in itself, fixed and immutable, the deficiency would cease and there would be no consciousness of absolute being; in the same manner, in the infinite infinitesimal fluctuation of variations there is nothing that can have consciousness of this fluctuation.

1. *But the will is at every point a will for determinate things.* And as it is deprived by time of *consisting* at every point, so it is deprived of persuasion at every point. *There is no possession of any thing*—only *changing with regard* to a thing, *entering into a relation* to a thing. Each thing *has* inasmuch as *it is had.*

2. *Determinacy is an attribution of value: consciousness.* Each thing at every point does not possess but is the will for determinate possession: that is, a determinate attribution of value: a determinate consciousness. At that point of the present when it enters *into a relation* with a given thing, it believes it is in the act of possession, but it is only a finite *potenza,* 'power,' 'potency': *finita potestas denique cuique,* 'each thing has

a limited power' (Lucr. I, 70).[17] In the ἄβιος βίος, 'lifeless life,' potency and act are one and the same, for the *transcendent Act*, "only the whole of eternity assembled," that is, *persuasion*, denies time and the will in every deficient moment.

*L'attualità*, 'presentness,' 'actuality'—every present moment, that which in every case and every manner is called life—is the infinitely various conjoining of *potency* finitely localized in infinitely various aspects—as consciousness, according to which in every case its correlate is stable amid the instability.

3. *Nothing is for itself but with regard to a consciousness.* Ἕως ἂν παρῇ μοι ἐλπίς τις—μένει μοί τι, 'if there is any hope at all for me, there is something for me'— for as long as I want in some manner, attribute value to some thing, there is something for me.

4. *Life is an infinite correlativity of consciousnesses.* The sense of life ἀλλοιοῦται ὅκωσπερ ὁκόταν συμμιγῇ θυώματα θυώμασιν, 'varies as when one mixes fragrances with fragrances' (Heraclitus).*[18]

"There is an appointed time for everything. And there is a time for every will under the heavens. . . . I have seen what the god has given the sons of men with which to occupy themselves.[19] He has made everything appropriate in its time. He has also set the world in their heart, yet so that man will not attain† the

---

*θυώματα is added by Mullachius. It is perhaps not appropriate, because Heraclitus discusses how things are unstable to the eye when observed through smoke, because one column of smoke or two comingled present the same image to the eye. In any case Mullachius knows much more about it than I do.

†*Ne inveniat.* [The author has merely provided the Latin original for his translation "*non giunga,*" 'will not attain.'—Translators' note.]

work which god has made from top to bottom (in its entirety)" (Ecclesiastes 3).[20]

We isolate a single determination of the will, for example, the stomach of a body, as if it lived for its own self: the stomach is all hunger, the attribution of value to food, the consciousness of the world insofar as it is edible. But in living for itself, before eating, it will have the pain of death, and in eating it will kill itself. In the same manner, when two substances combine chemically, each satisfying the determinacy of the other, each departs from its nature, altered in reciprocal absorption. *Their life is suicide.* Chlorine, for example, has always been so gluttonous that it is completely dead, but if we bring it back to life by placing it in the *proximity* of hydrogen, it lives only for the hydrogen. Hydrogen is the single value of the world to it: the world; its life is uniting with hydrogen.* And this is the light for every atom of the chlorine in its brief life on the *proximate* way to interpenetration. But once love is satisfied, *that light too shall be extinguished,* and the world shall be finished for the atom of chlorine. For the presence of the hydrogen atom will have become the *eyelid* to the chlorine atom's eye, which before saw nothing but hydrogen, and it will have covered the horizon for it, which before was all hydrogen. Their love is not for the satisfied life, not for being persuaded, but for the mutual need that ignores another's life. Their two worlds

---

*Chemists call the disposition of a substance toward conjunction with another "valency." This is well put: valency is the correlate of value (*sapore,* 'taste'—*sapienza,* 'knowledge'; *sentore,* 'feeling'—*sentenza,* 'judgment'). It changes little to say that chlorine might have valency for other substances as well. Let us suspend our erudition and suppose (for five minutes!) that it wants to know nothing but hydrogen; or rather, to silence our overly scrupulous, indoctrinated conscience, let us call all things that are valuable to chlorine *hydrogen.*

were diverse but correlative, so that from their mortal embrace something new would await and suffer life: chloric acid.

The one determination asserts itself in the self-assertion of the other, for each has seen in the other only its own self-assertion. Their love is hatred as their life is death.

Before their embrace the chloric acid was predetermined in the consciousness of the chlorine and of the hydrogen, and after, the chlorine and hydrogen exist in the consciousness of the chloric acid, which they determined; and the hydrogen, chlorine, and chloric acid—determined thus as they are and where they are for self-asserting and nonself-asserting—in the consciousness of all other things.

Whether or when the affirmation (the embrace) occurs is indifferent. *The correlativity is always and equally entire and infinite in the actuality running in time; past and future are in it; occurrence and nonoccurrence are indifferent.*

Ὁ Ἡράκλειτος γάρ φησιν, ὅτι καὶ τὸ ζῆν καὶ τὸ ἀπο-θανεῖν καὶ ἐν τῷ ζῆν ἡμᾶς ἐστι καὶ ἐν τῷ τεθνάναι, 'Indeed, says Heraclitus, living and dying are in our living and our dying.'[21]

But for the given quantity of chlorine it is a matter of life and death. From the moment when its *mortal life* came into being in whatever manner, it had a chloric consciousness; it despairingly hoped in its continuous deficiency because its eye *looked at the darkness* and saw nothing for itself: its life was *mortal pain.* If we now place hydrogen in its proximity, a distant, indistinct light appears to it in the obscurity, and it reawakens to a sharper hope in the twilight until, the hydrogen having come into the given proximity, the chlorine views the horizon as *completely clear* and affirms its now *certain life*—in the *mortal pleasure* of the embrace.

The hydrogen distant, it lacked everything and did not see what it lacked; it wanted and did not know what it wanted. Once the hydrogen comes in contact with it, becoming contingent to it, then *the chlorine wants the hydrogen.* This *contingency* is in the life of other things, which to the chlorine are obscure. It does not have a way to reach the hydrogen, cannot *procure itself* that nearness, does not have in itself the *certainty* of affirmation, but waits inert: time always preterits its will.[22] Chlorine does not want but would want,* because the condition necessary for its determinate wanting is not in itself but in what is a mystery to it, infinite obscurity, contingency of things, chance: it is the consciousness of other things. Through this sense of useless time the chlorine *grows bored* when distant from hydrogen.

But the will cannot stand boredom, and from the inert anticipation of nearness it moves, broadening its consciousness from the punctual determinacy across the infinite variety of forms: the determinations combine into complexes, because each time they must providently acquire the nearness through which each determination affirms itself little by little and does not remain dead, and continues through the power of the complex in order once again to affirm itself. The stomach is not hungry for its own sake *but for the body.*

The stomach is absorbed by eating. But the body, all while being intent on eating, is not absorbed by it. The former exhausts both the food and itself inasmuch as it is all hunger; the latter, exhausting its hunger by eating, has better hope of continuing. The satisfaction of the determinate deficiencies al-

---

*Indeed the indicative: *voglio,* 'I want'; the conditional: *ebbi a volere,* 'I had to want'—*vorrebbi*—*vorrei,* 'I would want.' [*Vorrebbi* is based on an obsolete Tuscan variant of the first-person conditional. In Tuscan the endings correspond to the past perfect forms of *avere.*—Translators's note.]

lows the complex of determinations to remain deficient. The complex calls itself satiated in this respect without being completely satiated, because the *criterion* of that determination's self-affirmation is *the foresight of the others:* the complex of determinations is not chaos but an *organism.*

In the indifferent haze of things the god *makes* the one thing the organism needs *shine;* and the organism struggles toward it as if to satiate all its hunger, as if that thing could provide all its life: *absolute persuasion.* But the knowing god extinguishes the light when its abuse would remove its usefulness, and the animal, satiated only with regard to that thing, turns toward another light, which the benevolent god has shown it. And toward it the organism struggles with all its hope, until again the light is extinguished, only to be reignited at another point. . . . No sooner does the animal feel disappointed, the thread of its existence having been cut short, than the light reappears without respite like lightning on a summer night. And in that light *the animal's entire future gleams:* the possibility of eating, sleeping, drinking, lying together shines in the pursuit of another animal, while in eating lies the possibility of running, resting, and so on.

In this manner, flattering the animal with arguments for its own life, the wise god leads it across the obscurity of things in his luminous wake in order that the animal should *continue and never be persuaded*—until an obstacle puts an end to the sad game.

This benevolent and prudent god is the god of philopsychia* and the *light* is *pleasure.*[23]

For this reason each animal comes determinately into contact with the things of its determinate love, and although

*Love of life, cowardice.

these things are in its future, it does not see the whole work the
god has made. Because if it saw

> as in a single moment
> ice and the rose, great cold and burning heat,[24]

it would not clutter its soul

> before, now, tomorrow, morning and evening;[25]

it would not continue in time because, as people say, "He who
sees God must die."

But its will-to-be is directed toward continuing insofar
as its present self-affirmation creates the next nearness for the
self-affirmation of another determination: each contains the
foresight of the others. The will feeds on the future in each
empty present, and as it assures itself of the former by means
of the evident signs of the latter, it provides for the future *sine
cura,* now affirming itself confidently.

An ox never pecks at wheat but only chews the cud of
hay; nor does it ever get indigestion from the hay: thus does
*pleasure guide* it. It does not like wheat but finds hay sweet, yet
only as long as the hay suits it. The ox finds suitable what
pleases it for as long as it is pleased. And the voice of all the
other determinations saying that thing in that measure necessary to its continuation speaks in the sweetness. The promised
sweetness of the future, the determinations of other things, the
foresight of the given future, all live in the present *taste* of
the hay. Through the taste it knows what is good for it,* what
makes its continuation possible, bringing the realization of the

---

*Sapio = ho sapore = so, 'I taste = I have taste = I know.'

continuous turning of its needs gradually closer. *In the taste lies the presence of its entire persona.* This *taste* accompanies *every act of organic life,* for which reason Ecclesiastes says (3:12): "I know there is nothing better for them (according to them) than to take pleasure in it, and it does them good in their life; and moreover man sees the good in eating, drinking, and in all his labor—this is given to him by god."

Thus, as he moves in the turning of things that give him pleasure, man pivots on the fulcrum given (προϋπάρχει)[26] to him by god and attends to his own continuation without *troubling about it,* because pleasure troubles the future for him.

He finds this sweet taste in each thing, which he feels as *his own* because it is useful for his continuation, and in each, affirming himself with its potency, he draws from it the flattery "*You are.*"

So that, time after time, in the *presentness of his affirmation,* he feels superior to the present moment and to the relation belonging to it; and if he does this now and that later, this here and that there, he always feels the same amid diverse times and things: he says, "*I am.*"

And at the same time *his* things, which surround him and await his future, are the *only reality,* absolute and indisputable—with its good and bad, its better and worse. He does not say, "This is for me" but "This is"; he does not say, "I like this" but "It's good," because in fact the I for whom the thing is or is good is his *consciousness, his pleasure,* his *presentness,* which for him is fixed, absolute, outside time. *It is him* and *is* the world. And the things of the world *are* good or bad, useful or harmful; he knows how "to refuse the evil and choose the good" (Isaiah),[27] because his presentness in pleasure (or displeasure) has *organized the foresight* of what is suitable to the organism's continuation, which creates from afar the future proximity necessary to the future affirmation. For this reason things are not indifferent but subject to judgment with regard *to an end.* This end, which is in his consciousness, is indisputable to him, fixed, luminous among the indifferent things. What he *does* is not random but *certain and reasonably subordinate* to the end. Just as he says, "I am," so he says, "I know what I *do* because I do it; I don't act by chance but with full consciousness and persuasion." *Thus does what lives persuade itself that whatever life it lives is life.*

ii

But the world is fixed for only so long as man remains on his feet, and man remains on his feet only so long as the world has a foundation. Μένει γὰρ αὐτῷ ἅπερ ἂν αὐτὸν μένῃ, 'reality for him is what anticipates his future.'

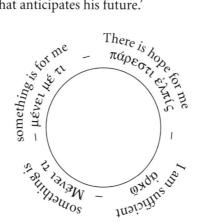

This is the exitless circle of illusory individuality, which affirms a *persona,* an end, a reason: *inadequate persuasion,* in that it is adequate only to the world it creates for itself. The world of each is *the* world; and that world's value is the correlative of its *valency*, its *sapore*, 'flavor,' the correlative of his *knowledge*. My world is but my correlative: my pleasure. Hence says the philosopher, ὀνομάζεται καθ᾽ ἡδονὴν ἑκάστου, 'it is said according to the pleasure of each individual' (Heraclitus).[28] Each *knows* what he *wants*, sees what he *lives*, what distant things his pleasure approaches in looking ahead. He *comprehends* what he *can grasp*.

*My life and the world I live are one and the same.*

Thus says Parmenides: τωὐτόν ἐστι νοεῖν τε καὶ οὕνεκέν ἐστι νόημα, 'the thought and the thing I think are one and the same.'[29]

His *certain end*, his *reason for being*, the *sense* that each act has for him, again are nothing but his self-continuation. The illusory *persuasion* according to which he wills things as valid in themselves and acts as if toward a certain end and affirms himself as an individual with reason in himself is none other than *the will of himself in the future*. He neither sees nor wants anything but himself: ἄνθρωπος ἐν εὐφρόνῃ φάος ἅπτει ἑαυτῷ, 'man ignites a light for himself in the darkness' (Heraclitus).[30]

But while lacking himself in the present he wills himself in the future—which he *cannot* do but along the way of singular determinations organized so as to make him continue wanting in such a manner in the future. He circles around the way of singular needs and escapes himself always. He cannot *possess himself*, have reason for himself, inasmuch as it is *necessary* for him to attribute value to his own *persona*, which is determined in things, and to the things he needs in order to continue. For by such things he is *distracted in time* along the way.[31] His coming to mortal life, his birth, is in the will of others; the fulcrum on which he turns is given him, and given him are the things he calls his own. For he does not have them any more than he himself is had, even provided that in the organization of determinations his own self-affirming consciousness is not absorbed.

But his *power in things is limited* at each point to *a limited foresight.* From the relation to the thing he draws not possession but the security of his own life—*but this too lies in a brief, finite circle;* and the *brevity of the horizon is present at every point in the superficiality of the relation.* Thus as the possession of the thing escapes him, so escapes the mastery *of his own life,* which cannot affirm itself infinitely but only in relation to the finite circle, which cannot rest in the present but is drawn by time to self-affirmation within limits ever ahead of it; neither can he, by more turning, grasp more from things and attain actual self-possession—*persuasion*–by the possession of them. Thus does the god of philopsychia, in flattering him, *make sport of him.*

And man, all while rejoicing in the affirmation, senses that this *persona* is not his, that he does not possess it. And beyond the circle of his foresight, which procures the nearness of the given distance, which overcomes the given contingencies to which his *persona* is sufficient, he senses other infinite wills, in the contingency of which the things inside his consciousness still find themselves and inside which his future is contained.

Below the superficiality of his pleasure he senses the flow of what is outside his power and transcends his consciousness. The known (finite) weave of illusory individuality, where pleasure casts its light, is not so tight that the obscurity of the (infinite) unknown does not penetrate. And his pleasure is contaminated by a *dull and continuous pain,* whose voice is indistinct, which the thirst for life represses in the turning of determinations. Men fear pain and to avoid it apply the poultice of *faith* with a force adequate to the infinity of the power they do not know, and they entrust it with the weight of the pain they cannot bear. The god they honor, to whom they give everything, is the god of philopsychia, a well-known god, cherished, affable, familiar. They pay the other god created by them to take charge of what appears to the individual as *chance* in that it transcends his power, and to watch over the house while they are feasting, and to change everything for the better. This too has been skillfully engineered by the familiar god in order to have better control over men. "If you are here," he whispers in everyone's ear, "you are certainly here for the better, and it is timely that Providence put you in this world made for you and looks after your security here, and as long as you live content, don't worry about it."

But the dull voice of obscure pain still is not quiet, and again and again it rules, alone and terrible, in the fearful hearts of men.

When the light dims, the image of dear things—the screen veiling the external obscurity—becomes more tenuous, and the invisible grows visible; when the weave of illusion thins, disintegrates, tears asunder, then men, *made impotent,* feel themselves in the sway of what is *outside their power, of what they do not know: they fear without knowing what they fear. They find themselves wanting to flee death, having lost their usual way, which feigns finite things from which to flee all while seeking finite things.*

The weave of children—provisional lives, so to speak— is much less defined, much more varied and disordered, here dense and luminous, there thin and half-dark, half-translucent. They have living joys men no longer know and are much more often than men in the grip of such terrors. In the intervals of

their undertakings and plans, when they are alone and not
drawn by anything surrounding them to rummage, steal, break,
argue, or engage in any of their other occupations, they find
themselves *watching the obscurity* with their little minds. Things
are deformed into strange appearances: watching eyes, listening ears, reaching arms, a sarcastic sneer, and everywhere danger. They feel watched by terribly powerful beings who mean
them ill. They no longer make a single gesture without thinking of "them." If they do something with one hand, they must
do it with the other. "Or should I not do it?" they think. "'They'
want me to do it—but I won't, I won't obey—but what if I'm
not doing it just because I'm thinking of 'them'—so maybe I
should do it. . . ." Passing by a dark room, it seems to children
that "they" scream in a thousand voices and grab them with
a thousand hands, and sarcasm sneers in the obscurity with a
thousand quivers, and they feel sucked in by the obscurity;
they run, wild with terror, screaming to stupefy themselves.

But then life takes charge of the stupefying: being alive
becomes a habit; *things that don't attract are no longer watched;*
the others are tightly linked; the weave becomes smooth—the
child becomes a man. The fearful hours are reduced to the
dull, continuous, measured pain trickling beneath all things.
But when the edge of the weave is lifted for reasons beyond
men's control, they too know frightful moments. Dreams
come to them in sleep, when the organism, relaxed, lives the
obscure pain of singular determinations, for which, in the
thinning of the weave of illusion, the obscurity appears more
menacing. Ἄνθρωπος ἐν εὐφρόνῃ φάος ἅπτει ἑαυτῷ· ἀπο-
θανὼν ἀποσβεσθείς. Ζῶν δὲ ἅπτεται τεθνεῶτος εὕδων, 'man
ignites a light for himself in the darkness. It goes out as he dies.
But sleeping alive, he is similar to the dead' (Heraclitus).[32] Sarcastic laughter disturbs, ruins, corrupts the tranquil, familiar

images they would like to retain in vain, and it weighs upon them with dark images of menace and reproach; στάζει δ᾽ ἐν θ᾽ ὕπνῳ πρὸ καρδίας / μνησιπήμων πόνος· καὶ παρ᾽ ἄ / κοντας ἦλθε σωφρονεῖν, 'in the heart, recalled remorse, like a wound that bleeds, wakes in sleep; and wisdom is born though we reject it' (Aeschylus, *Agamemnon*).[33] They awake, open their eyes wide in the dark . . . , and the relieving match gives them peace—the sweet wife is just beside; here the clothes with the body's imprint, here in the pictures the familiar faces of loved ones; all the dear, dear, familiar things. "It's okay. Okay. What time is it? Oh! Late. Gotta get up tomorrow. Damn dreams. God, dreams! Okay. Tomorrow. Let's see if we can get right back to sleep." Reassured, they put out the light again, but the images remaining in the eyes decompose, the plans for tomorrow and the next day cease—man finds himself once more without first name and last, wife or loved ones, things to do, clothes. He is alone, naked, with eyes open to the darkness. Ἀποσβεσθεὶς ὄψεις ἐγρηγορὼς ἅπτεται εὕδοντος, 'the vision extinguished, waking he resembles one who sleeps' (Heraclitus).[34] Every sensation becomes infinite; it seems that before your eyes points draw infinitely away; small things become infinitely large, and *the infinite drinks them up;* in anguish you seek a plank with which to save yourself, a solid point; everything decomposes, everything yields, flees, draws away; and the sarcastic sneer dominates all: "Ooooooooooohhh . . . nothing, nothing, nothing, I know you're nothing; I know you're nothing; I know where you place your trust and I shall destroy the ground from under you; I know what you promise yourself and your promises won't be kept, just as you have promised and never kept, never kept—because you're nothing, and you can do nothing, I know you can do nothing, nothing, nothing. . . ." Time passes you by *ad infinitum* and preterits your will. You know the anguish of not having done and the anxiety of doing things in their proper time, while what you do not know approaches and presses you from all sides. You feel behind in time, dissolving like a corpse preserved in an airless environment, which no sooner than exposed turns to dust. You feel long dead and yet live and fear death. In the face of slowly advancing, inexorable time, you feel as powerless to care for your life as a dead man, and you suffer each moment the pain of death.* This pain is common to all things that live and do not have life in themselves, living without persuasion, fearing death in living. And no one recognizes it dripping from every moment of life, but calls it joy. Everyone, calling himself content and sufficient and satisfied in the light of morning, feels it absorbing him in the terrors of night and loneliness but does not admit it. But it rests in the opinions and mouths of everyone when it becomes apparent in specific events, when, as the *impotence* appears to be caused by determinate things, it too is deemed definite and limited; then it is called remorse, melancholy and boredom, rage, pain, fear, "excessive" joy.

*Remorse* for a determinate, given deed, which is not finite repentance for that deed alone but terror for one's own life destroyed in the irrevocable past (for which one feels alive and impotent in the face of the future), is the infinite distress that gnaws at the heart.

*Melancholy* and *boredom*, which men localize in things as if there were melancholic or boring things, are the same terror

*Upon the announcement of Orestes' death, which took away her reason for living (until then she had fixed her gaze on the future), Electra does not say rhetorically, "I feel I am dying," or "I am dying," but ὄλωλα τῇδ᾽ ἐν ἡμέρᾳ, 'I have perished this day'; and then with greater force: ἀπωλόμην δύστηνος, οὐδέν εἰμ᾽ ἔτι, 'I perished, wretched me, I am no longer anything' (Sophocles, *Electra* ll. 674, 676).

of the infinite, when the weave of illusion is in some manner interrupted, so that man senses the pain of nonbeing and feels lost, impotently wanting in the sway of the unknown.*

*Fear*, which men believe limited to a given danger, is rather the terror of the man who senses his impotence before the infinite obscurity: for he is carried outside his own power. The infinite time of impotency is evident to each: men die of fear, or if they do not die, age decades in minutes; and the destruction of the individual is evident in the fact that fear deprives him of every potency (Lucretius III, 157: *concidere ex animi terrore videmus / saepe homines*, 'oft we see, out of spiritual terror / men crumble');[35] consequently, he does not even do what he could—or he does the opposite. Not being able to bear the danger, men throw themselves into certain death, like hens stricken with terror at the passing of a bicycle who bolt from the safe edge of the road into the middle, squawk desperately before the wheels, and get themselves run over.†

*Occasions of melancholic boredom: (1) the *monotony* that exhausts the value of things for the individual, making time seem infinite; (2) the recognition of the other's individuality as illusory *whenever that individuality has clear contact with one's own* (otherwise the cart driver who travels through sleeping villages at night feels sorry for the men closed within a circle that for him has no value and rejoices in his heart for his certain destination—while on the other hand the man awake in a room of one of the village houses, happy at his laborious wakefulness or at his next repose, feels sorry for the obscure man on the road, who goes on and on and whose going has no end); (3) to see once more the traces of *one's own life*, which once was rich with infinite hope and then, through convenience, cowardice, adjustment, is now reduced, abandoned, sold out: traces of a life whose future was at any rate richer in time than at any point since.

†Disgust is none other than fear. One experiences disgust for the things that touch us or can touch us and before which we are impotent, though they may be weaker than we are. I have in mind the small, scurrying creatures that approach one in a disquieting manner and are soft or slimy or filthy to the touch, or swift in their swerving such as to be uncatchable. Dis-

*Rage,* powerless before the accomplished fact or the greater strength of another, feeds infinitely on itself, for which reason the philosopher says: χαλεπὸν θυμῷ μάχεσθαι· ψυχῆς γὰρ ὠνέεται, 'rage is difficult to resist; it is purchased at the cost of life' (Heraclitus).[36]

*Pain* of loss, of a determinate injury, which men believe limited to this alone, is rather terror at the revelation of the impotency of one's own illusion; it is a certain accident or malady, a death, ruin, catastrophe of given, familiar things: but it is mystery that opens the door to the tranquil, bright room warmed sufficiently for determinate hope, and it sneers: "Now I'm coming, and here you thought you were safe, and you are nothing."

Finally, *excessive joy,* which, putting everything one used to live for and value absolutely into the present, with a single stroke, takes away one's reason for living while not satiating entirely, making one continue to want without knowing what any longer: impotently.* And if the weave's rip made by the loss is sewn back up and men delude themselves again and readapt to some kind of life, excessive joy takes reason away for good, making one go crazy or die; hence it is said: ἐλαίου δέων ὁ λύχνος σβέννυται, ἐλαίου δὲ φλέοντος ἀπεσβέσθη, 'the lamp goes out for lack of oil, and for excess it is suffocated.'[37]

Everywhere the same pain of life that does not satiate it-

---

gust before ills, swooning at the sight of them, is characteristic of our impotency before them, which makes us feel them now.

*Lives pitched in *camp,* provisional (infants, soldiers, for whom the actuality of the good they hope is deferred for a fixed term by the will of another; and hope is therefore intact), having their elementary needs satisfied, their finite tasks accomplished: they do not know how to vent their joy. Hence youthful αὐθαδία, 'arrogance.' Wine that satisfies excessively has the same effect, creating the reality of any illusion of the moment.

self and believes it satiates itself, for it is rendered perspicuous by an individual consciousness's contingency on the flow of other consciousnesses, which makes the brief illusion aware of its impotence; and it finds itself wanting desperately, not resting on the given, safe things that anticipate its future.

And once the voice of pleasure, which tells it *you are*, is interrupted, it senses only the dull, painful murmur, now made distinct, which says: *you are not;* and all the while it asks for life.

## iii

The flower sees the propagation of its pollen in the bee, while the bee sees sweet food for its larvae in the flower. In the embrace of the two organisms each sees "itself as if in a mirror" (*Phaedro* 255d) in the disposition of the other. Neither knows whether its affirmation coincides with the other's or whether conversely its affirmation deprives the other of the future— killing it; each knows only that this is good for it and uses the other as a means to its own end, material for its own life, while it is itself the material for the other's life. Thus, the affirmation of illusory individuality, which violates things in affirming itself without persuasion (for it *informs them with its illusory goal as if with the goal of the absolute individual who has reason in himself*), takes on the appearance of love out of mutual necessity. But ἀντέρως,* 'reciprocated love,' is not ἔρως, 'love'; it is a travesty of νεῖκος, 'strife.'

And when coincidence does not provide for the continuation of both, when the cog of one large or small gear does not

---

*In using the word at the point cited, Plato has a different intention, just as in his use of the simile of the mirror. This matters little here and does not weaken the argument.

fit into the cavities of another or vice versa, *inimical violence*
manifests itself. For where one affirms itself the other cannot,
and if both do not perish in the struggle, one must concede or
succumb to the other, so that at once the impotence of the
minor power manifests itself.

The weak individual, whose life requires him to affirm
himself in habitual relation to one stronger than he, is like the
satyr before the hermaphrodite: he senses a definite lust and at
the same time feels that it is outside his power to procure the
nearness of the familiar act. He no longer touches bottom with
his sounding line but feels himself in the sway of an unknown
sea's waves, for in the other's eye he senses the obscurity of a
power that transcends him, an enigma full of menace for him;
he wants and no longer wants, and in his lust terror is depicted.*

The weaker one, he whom the stronger makes material
for his own life, is like a dove in the claws of a hawk. The weaker
one, who wants to affirm himself in the same place as the
stronger, is like an inexperienced shooter next to a hunter. The
latter has the nearness of the distant animal *in* his hand and *in*
his sure eye; the former sees the animal in a distance that is as
infinite to his eye as it is ἄπορος, 'beyond the reach,' of his
hand. In his eyes he has an uncertainty of points, in his hand,
the weapon.

In a vaster consciousness the thing is more real because it
reflects that vaster life. The consciousness *has* that thing in a
greater fashion because in its affirmation there are means of a
foresight more organized toward a vaster life, a foresight suffi-

---

*The group statue of the satyr and the hermaphrodite that I have in
mind is at the Uffizi Gallery in Florence, I believe; it is a Greek work. The hermaphrodite's head may not be the original and may have been replaced by
the head of some divinity, but by this substitution perhaps the quiet assur-
ance in the whole attitude of the youth is more evident. There is something
similar, though weaker, in the Christ looking at Judah by Titian.

cient to eliminate a greater vastness of contingencies and in
which *a greater distance has certainty, finitude, proximity at any
given moment.*

It is as when two men play chess and the same pieces are
not the same for each because to one they have a great circle of
possibilities linked one to another so as to be sufficient, in vast
foresight, to all the opponent's possible moves; to the other,
assuming that he is inferior, they are reduced to a brief circle
of moves that can only connect with a small, local plan, whereas the moves of the former are an incomprehensible contingency to him, because of which he gradually sees his little plans
undermined and is forced to start again, adapting himself to
each new situation.

*Thus in life do the weak adapt.* And to this they are led by
the god of philopsychia: "You want this? You've devoted yourself to getting it? It doesn't matter. Give in. When you can't get
it, when life is at stake, the thing you wanted *here,* you can have
it somewhere else after all, in some other way, with the same
pleasure, and without danger."

Indeed, one can repeat that superficiality of relations in-
differently in another manner and another place. The less deep
the life of an organism, the less is its reason for affirming itself
in relation to these things, in this moment, in this environment. It can continue with regard to other things in another
environment, provided it is offered the possibility of the relations necessary to its continuation. Its palate knows only crass
distinctions. It does not live things more profoundly but affirms in them only its superficial relations, its small world. And
the smaller its world, the more indifferent, easily reproducible,
and transplantable it is among different things. One takes the
fish with a little *of the water from where it lives* and tosses it into
other water; the plant, not with naked roots but *with just that*

*much* soil, and puts it in a vase; a man, *with the means of subsistence,* and makes of him whatever one wants.

He who does not live with *persuasion cannot fail to obey, for he has already obeyed.* Πρὸς τὸν βίον παντοῖος γίγνεται φιλοψυχίᾳ πειθόμενος ὅστις ὁρμᾶται ἄνευ πειθοῦς, 'reaching for life, he who lives without persuasion assumes every form, obeying the fear of death.'

This, which men often call docility, goodness, or even superiority or knowledge of the world, is none other than the superficiality of those without reason in what they do, who merely *find themselves doing it,* not knowing why they wanted the things they wanted, having neither the potency of those things in themselves nor the sufficiency to withstand their loss. Instead they find themselves extracting their little lives from those things. Only fear for their own continuation makes them exchange those things now, in the same way that they grasped them before, when they obeyed that fear through insufficiency.

# III
# The Way to Persuasion

TRANSLATORS' NOTE: *Facing one's fear of death is the beginning of wisdom. What Heidegger, in* Being and Time, *was to call Being-toward-death is the condition of being persuaded, being fully present to oneself. Sophocles is seen as affirming this wisdom and Socrates and Jesus as actually living it out in their deaths.*

*Intertextually, we see the appearance of Hegel's master-slave dialectic in Michelstaedter's text: what was projected onto chemicals is now applied to the psychic life of humans. The essence of the difference between master and slave is that the slave prefers his own physical existence—he is addicted to philopsychia—even at the cost of being an inferior and living a life of frustration, whereas the master acquires his superiority precisely because of his willingness to preserve his integrity by dying. The difference can be seen in terms of how one handles fear of death. "He who fears death is already dead." The slave is dominated by fear, and so already dead, because he is attached to life (philopsychia). From this follows a whole catalogue of morbid pathic states or emotions: remorse, melancholy, despair, fear, rage, pain, excessive joy or giddy hilarity. The master, by contrast, embraces pain because he is indifferent to life or death and so escapes these negative states. It is impossible to forget that Michelstaedter's imminent suicide takes place against this background.*

*Κύριός εἰμι θροεῖν ὅδιον κράτος αἴσιον ἀνδρῶν ἐκτελέων·*

*ἔτι γὰρ θεόθεν καταπνείει πειθώ.*

*I have mastery to chant the wonder at the wayside / given to*

*kings. For from the gods persuasion surges within me.*

—Aeschylus[38]

Tί τοῦτο ποιεῖς, 'what you do,' how do you do it? In what state of mind? Do you love this thing for the correlation of what later leaves you needing the same correlation, whose proximity you foresee only to a given limit, so that, slave to the contingency of this correlation, you are deprived of all when the correlation is removed from the thing, and you must seek some other thing and place yourself under the sway of its contingency?

Or is it that *you know what* you do, and what you do, which is all inside you at the point of your doing it, cannot be taken away by anyone?

Are you persuaded of what you do or not? Do you need something to happen or not in order to do what you do? Do you need the correlations to coincide always, because the end is never in what you do, even if what you do is vast and distant but is always in your continuation? Do you say you are persuaded of what you do, no matter what? Yes? Then I tell you: tomorrow you will certainly be dead. It doesn't matter? Are you thinking about fame? About your family? But your memory dies with you, with you your family is dead. Are you thinking about your ideals? You want to make a will? You want a headstone? But tomorrow those too are dead, dead. All men die with you. Your death is an unwavering comet. Do you turn to god? There is no god, god dies with you. The kingdom of heaven crumbles with you, tomorrow you are dead, dead. Tomorrow *everything* is finished—your body, family, friends, country, what you're doing now, what you might do in the future, the good, the bad, the true, the false, your ideas, your little part, god and his kingdom, paradise, hell, everything, everything, everything. Tomorrow everything is over—in twenty-four hours *is death.*

Well, then the god of today is no longer yesterday's, no longer the country, the good, the bad, friends, or family. You want to eat? No, you cannot. The taste of food is no longer the same; honey is bitter, milk is sour, meat nauseating, and the odor, the odor sickens you: *it reeks of the dead.* You want a woman to comfort you in your last moments? No, worse: *it is dead flesh.* You want to enjoy the sun, air, light, sky? Enjoy?! The sun is a rotten orange, the light extinguished, the air suffocating. The sky is a low, oppressive arc. . . . No, everything is closed and dark now. But the sun shines, the air is pure, everything is like before, and yet you speak like a man buried alive, describing his tomb. And persuasion? You are not even persuaded of the sunlight; you cannot move a finger, cannot remain standing. The god who kept you standing, made your day clear and your food sweet, gave you family, country, paradise—he betrays you now and abandons you because the thread of your philopsychia is broken.

The meaning of things, the taste of the world, is only for continuation's sake. Being *born* is nothing but wanting to go on: men live in order to live, in order *not to die.* Their persuasion is *the fear of death.* Being *born* is nothing but *fearing death,* so that, if death becomes certain in a certain future, *they are already dead in the present.* All that they do and say with fixed persuasion, a clear purpose, and evident reason is nothing but fear of death–σοφὸν γὰρ εἶναι δοκεῖν μὴ ὄντα—οὐδὲν ἄλλο ἐστὶ ἢ θάνατον δεδιέναι, 'indeed, believing one is wise without being wise is nothing but fearing death.'*

Every present in their lives contains death. Their lives are nothing but fear of death. They live in order to save what is given them in birth, as if they had been born with persuasion and the choice of death were within them. What is given them is nothing but fear of death, and this, as sufficient life, they wish to rescue from what was also given them then: the certainty of dying. In these straits, and out of concern for a future that cannot help but repeat the present (for as long as it will repeat it), they pollute *the present,* which is in their hands. And where is life if not in the *present?* If this has no value nothing does.

*He who fears death is already dead.*

He who for one instant wants his life to be *his,* only for an instant to be persuaded of what he does, must take possession of the present, *to see every present as the last,* as if death were certain afterward, *and to create his own life by himself in the obscurity.* Death takes nothing from him who has his life in the present, because nothing in him asks to continue any longer; nothing in him exists merely through the fear of death—nothing is merely because it was given by birth as necessary to life. *And death takes nothing but what is born. It takes*

---

*Plato, *Apology,* but inverted: "θάνατον γὰρ δεδιέναι οὐδὲν ἄλλο ἐστὶ ἢ σοφὸν εἶναι δοκεῖν μὴ ὄντα," 'indeed, fearing death is none other than believing oneself wise without being wise.' [Plato, *Apology* 29a.—Translators' note.]

*nothing but what it took on the very day one was born,* the
one who, because he was born, lives in fear of death, for the
sake of living, because he lives—because he was born. But he
who wants to have his life must not believe that he was born,
and is alive, only because he was born. Nor must he believe his
life sufficient and therefore to be continued and defended
from death.

The needs and necessities of life are not necessities to
him, for he does not find it necessary to continue the life which,
lacking everything, turns out not to be *life.* He cannot take the
*persona* of these needs as sufficient if in fact they are concerned
with nothing but the future: he cannot affirm himself in the affirmation of those needs, which are given within him—just as
correlativity is given—by a contingency beyond and before
him. He cannot move, unlike the things that *are* in order for
him to *have need* of them. There is no bread for him, no water,
bed, family, country, or god—*he is alone in the desert* and must
create everything for himself: god, country, family, water,
bread. Otherwise, the needs that need points out to him *become his very need;* those remain ever distant because his need
to continue always projects them forward into the future. And
he will *never have* them, and whenever he goes toward them,
they will pull away: he chases his own shadow.

No, he must *permanere,* 'remain,' not follow those needs,
imagining them as fixed so that they should continue to attract
him into the future; he must remain even though he wants
them to be in the present, truly his. He must tirelessly *resist* the
current of his own illusion; if he gives in at one point and concedes to what concedes to him, his life again dissolves and he
lives his own death. For in accepting the sufficiency of his
need, which fear of death has determined, he affirms his own

insufficiency and seeks support for his life from others, taking on the *persona* of hunger in order to be hungry again in the next moment, whereas this moment should have been his last. In vain does he seek to deceive the remorse, the death of self he senses, through pleasure; beneath the pleasure the shadow of blind, mute pain remains, making it bitter and empty for him. In vain does he attempt thus to take possession of what attracted him. For the correlativity is finished and not within him, while the remainder sinks into shadow.

He who firmly wants his life does not make do, fearing to suffer, with that empty pleasure that would screen him from the pain, so that the pain might continue below, *blind, mute,* elusive; instead, he *takes on the persona of that pain* and bearing λύπης ἀντίρροπον ἄχθος, 'the correlative weight of pain' (Sophocles, *Electra*),[39] affirms himself where others are annihilated by the mystery; for he has the courage to tear away the weave of sweet and cherished things, which coddles one into the future, and he demands *real possession of the moment.* What is mystery to others because it transcends their power is not mystery to him who has willed it and affirmed himself in it. Thus must he *create himself* to have individual value, not moving, unlike the things that come and go, but being *persuaded* in himself.

But men say, "That's fine, but *in the meantime,* in the meantime you've got to live." "*In the meantime*"! What meantime? In the old days in Veneto they used to sing,

We hope stones
turn to loaves
so the poor
can eat them.

We hope water
turns to champagne
because no one grumbles
when he's rejoicing.

We hope, hoping
the time will come
when we all fall apart
so we won't hope anymore.

That's exactly it! But it is a question of life, yours, everyone's; there is no rest for the man who is in the current; every
instant of rest is the way back; no rest for the man who carries
a weight upward, for when he puts it down he will have to
return and pick it up again where it will have sunk: each rest is
a loss; he must retravel the road as much as he rests on it.
Everyone at every point of life ἐνταῦθ᾽ <ἐστίν> / ἵν᾽ οὐκέτ᾽
ὀκνεῖν καιρός, ἀλλ᾽ ἔργων ἀκμή, 'finds himself where / it is no
longer the opportune moment to hesitate, but to act' (Sophocles, *Electra*).[40]

They are like the man who dreams about getting up and
when he realizes that he is still lying down does not get up but
goes back to dreaming about getting up—so that, neither getting up nor ceasing to dream, he continues to suffer from the
living image that disturbs the peace of sleep and from the immobility that renders vain the action he is dreaming about.

They say, "We're neither first nor last in this world, and
since one's got to live, it's better to adapt yourself to what you
find, which you can't change anyway."

But *each is the first and the last*,[41] and he finds nothing
done before him. Nor is it to his advantage to trust that anything will be done after him. He must take on himself the re-

sponsibility for his life (as it must be lived in order for him to attain life), which cannot rest with another. He must have in himself the certainty of his own life, which others cannot give him. He must create himself and the world, which does not exist before him: he must be master and not slave in his house. And why should he do this? In anticipation of what? Preserving himself for what should he renounce the *present possession of his life* and destroy forever the way to *persuasion*? What would death take away from him that it has not already taken?

"But," they say, "my legs are weak, and that way of yours is impracticable."

Some are lame and some able, but man must make his own legs for walking and forge a path when there is no road. Along the usual ways men travel in a circle with no beginning or end; they come, go, compete, throng like busy ants, change places, certainly, since no matter how much they walk, they are always where they were before, because one place is as good as another in the valley without exit. Man must make himself a way to succeed in life and not move about among others, to bring others with him and not ask for prizes that may or may not be found along the ways of men.

"It's hard enough for each of us to carry his own cross and here you come and impose the unbearable, taking away the solaces we have a right to."

You do not carry the cross. Instead you are all crucified on the timber of your sufficiency, which is given to you, and the more you insist, the more you bleed: it suits you to say you carry the cross like a sacred duty, whereas you are heavy with the inert weight of your necessities. Have the courage not to admit those necessities and lift yourselves up for your own sakes. . . . But for you it is against those necessities that the possible and impossible are measured, the bearable and unbearable duties necessary to obtain your lives in peace. When you conform to the ways of the body, family, city, religion, you say, "I perform my *duties** as a man, son, citizen, Christian," and against these duties you measure your rights. But the account does not square.

What happens to this account is an odd story. If you set out with someone to reckon his brother's accounts,[42] you will easily come up with fixed results. Satisfied, you go show them to the brother to verify, and you see marvels of rage and abuse. You apologize, offer to do them again with him and, if he is softened and agrees, you shortly have a new result with the same ease, analogous to the first. But as far as verifying goes, you see that the values are inevitably inverted. . . . Right then you are led to think you are dealing with a reciprocal equation; and to find a new determinant you go to the third brother; but he laughs in your face, and instead of resolving the problem you present to him, he lays out an entirely new story. If you raise an objection, he gets angry. You go along—and come out with a third result with a pile of new variables. Besides the reciprocal duties between the first two brothers you have those between the first and third and the second and third, between the first and the other two, the second and the other two, the third and the other two. Have the other two look at the problem separately and you will have new rage, new abuse, and new results. You are disconcerted because the outcome is truly pitiful and unheard-of in the experience of the most proven mathematician. You started with a simple addition, and now after

---

*The English say, "I *shall* do" (*io* devo *fare*, 'I *must* do,' 'it is necessary with respect to an absolute reason that I do') in order to say, "*io farò*," 'I'll do'; and "you *will* do," and so on (*tu* vuoi *fare*, 'you *want* to do,' and so on, 'you have a kind of whim to do' something) in order to say, "*tu farai*," 'you'll do,' and so on.

many tiring calculations you have three third-degree equations and six variables. For the greater dignity of mathematics (and yourself), you conclude that you are faced with an "indeterminate" equation. Indeed, most indeterminate. If you make a further attempt, to your indignation you obtain—without counting the abuse—four fourth-degree equations and twelve variables. You dare to continue and, to your horror, you get a problem with five fifth-degree equations and thirty-five variables. The thing starts to worry you, especially because the determining equations are becoming uncertain and full of gaps. . . . You *almost* begin to question mathematics. But then, if you are a pure-bred mathematician, you go at it once more armed with every artifice, for you have been provoked. But in vain: you are lost in a fog of determinations with an infinite number of variables and an infinite exponent, irreducible, no matter how much you try: a truly most indeterminate equation, this matter of rights and duties between two brothers. Poor mathematicians, when you have to look for the data because they are not given—so much vain effort, and when the data are provided—so much useless work!

Is it possible that dear Sextus Empiricus, so immune to mathematics, was correct after all?[43]

It is better to think less about equations and more about *equity.*

Many are slaves to the line "one must live," expecting everything from the future and reaching out for things. They demand the usual relations from these as if they had a sufficient *persona* which, having reason in itself, had the right to demand. Everyone says, "But I've got a right too, after all"; "If you knew what I've suffered, you'd understand I'm right"; "One's got to try! Put yourself in my shoes and then judge!" And indeed, indeed, everyone is right—everyone can show you how the causes, the needs behind his act or demand, result as mathematically just: the stone is right in falling when the earth attracts it; the oppressed ant is right in protesting when the stone weighs on it; the mosquito is right in sucking man's blood when hunger drives it; man is right in killing it when it stings him; fleas are right, too, as are rabid dogs, leaf-lice, the plague, customs officers, police officers: everybody has the right to live—everyone who's had the fault of being born. You say, "We'll work it out, there's space for everybody." Yes, "*Good* Toby took the fly carefully, opened the window, and so on."[44] But seal up *good* Toby in the dark with mice, scalopendrids, scorpions, horseflies, and malarial mosquitoes, and you will see what *good* Toby takes up with his delicate fingers!

Πράξας γὰρ εὖ πᾶς ἀνὴρ ἀγαθός.
. . . ἄνδρα δ᾽ οὐκ ἔστι μὴ οὐ κακὸν ἔμμεναι,
ὃν ἀμάχανος συμφορὰ καθέλῃ.

Each man is good if he is well.
. . . but it is impossible not to be bad
for the man who has been stricken by irreparable
   misfortunes.

                                        Simonides[45]

*Alle haben recht—niemand ist gerecht:* 'Everyone is right—no one *has the right*.'[46] Because there is no effect without a cause, everything in the world is right to happen; each effect is just to its cause, each affirmation is just to its need. But no one *is just*: no one, for insofar as someone demands an affirmation that accords with his causes and needs, he *takes on their persona,* and he cannot have the *persona of justice*. If he is the son of certain causes and needs, he does not have *reason* in himself; and the affirmation of whichever *persona* he has is always, because irrational, *violent*. In whatever manner he asks to continue, the necessities of his existence speak in him, and insofar as he affirms as *just* what *is just to him*, he denies what is just to others, and he is unjust toward *all* others, whether he wrongs them or not.*

"Surely there is not a just man on earth, who does good and commits no wrong" (Ecclesiastes).[47] Πᾶς ἄνθρωπος πρὸς βίον πανοῦργος—ὅστις γὰρ θάνατον δέδιε τὸ ἑαυτοῦ μέρος παντὶ ἄδικός ἐστιν, 'each man is dishonest before life—for he who fears death is, for his part, unjust toward all.' The good, pious, honest, just, beneficent, living men are as unjust toward others as they are dead in themselves. For they content themselves with living without persuasion out of fear of death; their every act and word is unjust and dishonest for it is always the affirmation of an illusory individuality.

Justice, the just *persona*, the individual with reason in himself is a hyperbole, people will say, *turning back to life as if they possessed it*—but the way of persuasion leading to that justice is hyperbolic. Indeed, just as the hyperbola approaches the asymptote infinitely, so does the man who wants his life while living infinitely approach the axis of justice; no matter how short the distance of a point of the hyperbola from the asymptote, the curve must extend itself infinitely in order to attain contact. Likewise, however little man, in living, demands as just to himself, his duty toward justice remains infi-

*Compare "*potenza*," 'potency' or 'power,' "*atto*," 'act,' "*attualità*," 'presentness' or 'actuality'; Part One, Chapter II.

nite. The right to live cannot be paid by finite labor, only by infinite activity.*

Because you participate in the violence of all things, all of
this violence is part of your debt to justice. All of your activity
must go toward eradicating this: *to give everything and demand
nothing;* this is the *duty*—where dut*ies* and right*s* may be, I do
not know.

*For the pleasure of mathematicians: let us take the special instance
in which the asymptotes function as coordinates: $x\,y = m^2$.

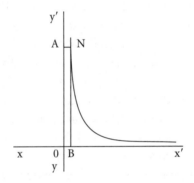

I say: $m^2$ (the constant) represents the constant space that man occupies in the world while continuing himself, while living as a thing among
things.

$x$ represents that which man demands as just for himself, the rights he
believes he has.

$y$ represents his *activity,* that which he gives, the duty he accomplishes.

$yy'$ represents the axis of justice.

Now one may discuss the formula: Let $C$ be the point of contact in the
infinite with $yy'$; so $\lim_0 x = 0$; $\lim_0 y = \infty$.

In the limit case, at the point of contact between justice and life, needs
are zero; activity is infinite: rational activity = *infinita potestas,* the *act.*

At point $N$: $x = x_n$, $y = y_n$;

$\lim_0 y - y_n = \infty - y_n = \infty$ corresponds to the difference

$\lim_0 x - x_n = 0 - x_n = -x_n$.

Through the choice of whatever thing man demands, beyond what

The activity that does not demand, that does not do in order to have but gives in doing, is benefaction.

Giving, doing, benefiting—three beautiful words. Everyone gives, does, benefits: but nobody has, nothing is done, and the good, who knows it?

1. *Giving is not for the sake of having given but for giving* (δοῦναι!). If I walk into a store and pay for the merchandise—this too is an act of "giving." But I pay for the merchandise and not for the pleasure of paying. If I could *have paid* and could keep the merchandise without paying, I would be satisfied. Paying is the means and not the end.

Munificence that expects recognition, beneficence that expects gratitude, sacrifice that expects reward, are just like any other affair that does not have the end in itself but is a means to having something, and being necessitated by the need of the latter, it depends for its future on the latter. Giving for the sake of having given is not giving but *demanding.*

*Doing* is not for the sake of having done; having done does no good. You do not have in the present what you have done, and yet you want to retain it. In order to have it you must *do it again* like anything else: and you don't reach an end. *Performing a beneficence* is not doing unto others or giving them

---

justice allows (that is, 0), his debt in activity, the duty he ought to fulfill and does not, is infinite.

In the limit case the constant is an infinite line, no longer a surface (one side being reduced to zero and the other being infinite): *the just man no longer lives,* does not continue himself but sates himself in the present. But in mathematics the limit is the point one infinitely approaches and never touches. Surely men have a more suitable criterion: they measure the sides of their lives and say, "An even swap—that's justice." But they fool themselves, for they do not have anything of what they ask, and what they give is nothing.

what they *believe they want:* giving alms, healing the sick, feeding, giving drink, clothing—these are *allowing others to take,* not giving or doing but *suffering.*[48]

2. He who *is* not cannot *do;* he who *has* not cannot *give;* he who *knows not the good* cannot *benefit:* this activity of finite beneficences is itself a form of *violence.* For while affirming itself as an individual activity, it is always a slave to what it wants to continue in the future. Irrational needs affirm themselves in such activity, demanding.

This is the easy, weak, stupid compassion of the *persona* who does not know what he is doing but wants to have the illusion of doing. If giving men the means of life were a just activity, then making children would be a divine thing.

Not giving men support against their fear of death but taking this fear away, not giving them illusory life and the means of always demanding it but giving them *life* here and now entirely so that they *do not demand*—this is the activity that eradicates the violence.

"That is impossible."

Certainly: impossible! For the *possible* is what is given. The possible are the needs, the necessities of continuing, what is within the limited power directed to continuation, in fear of death, what is death in life, the indifferent fog of things that are and are not. The courage of the impossible is the light that cuts the fog, before which the terrors of death fall away and the present becomes *life.* What do you care about living if you give up life in every present for the sake of the possible? if you are in the world and not in the world, grasping things without having them, eating things and remaining hungry, sleeping and remaining tired, loving and doing one another violence, if you are and are not?

3. *Giving is doing the impossible: giving is having.* For as

long as man lives, *he* is here, and the *world* is there. For as long
as *he* lives he wants to possess it. For as long as he lives he affirms himself in some manner. He *gives* and *demands.* He enters the ring of relations—and it is always *he here* and *there the
world, different from him.* Facing *that* which was once a given
relation for him, where in affirming himself he demanded to
continue, *now* he must affirm himself not in order to continue,
must love that not because it is necessary to his need but because of what it *is.* He must *give* all of *himself* to all of it in order
*to have it,* because in it he does not see a particular relation but
all the world, and in the face of this all, he is not his hunger,
torpor, need for affection, or any other of his needs—he is
everything: for in that final present he must have and give
everything: *to be persuaded and to persuade,* to have in the possession of the world the possession of oneself—*to be one with
the world.*

He must feel as if he is *in the desert* in the midst of the
self-offerings of particular relations, because in none of them
can he affirm all of himself. In each thing offering him these
relations,[49] he must love the life of the thing and not use the relation, *affirming himself without demanding.** But each thing's
life is not what it believes is just to itself, and he must not ask
for that from the things themselves and thus make himself an
instrument of their every demand,[†] because being just to one,
he would be unjust to the other: he would repeat the contingency of their consciousnesses. No, he himself must want them,
create them, *love in them all of himself, and in communicating
individual value, identify himself.*

---

*Everybody knows the first impression of a thing is the most just, the
freshest, and unrecoverable once the relation to it becomes habitual. It is because the first judgment was the affirmation that did not demand.

†"Eventual goodness."

But this all is never all and the affirmation is always a concession because infinite are the disguises of philopsychia.

He must not content himself until he is not content,* 
must not dispose himself to gathering the fruits of life in peace.
There are no respites on the way of persuasion. *Life is all one
long hard thing.*

He must have the *courage to feel alone,* to look his own
pain in the face, bearing the *entire* weight of it.

He must not content himself with what he has given,
even if others say they are content with it: he must see that even
though they say yes, their entire life that demands the future says
no. He has committed violence against them, even if they are
content with what is not valuable; and if he too is content with
that, not having the courage to deny it, again he *is dishonest.*

And this is not so in general but at every point. If he talks
to his friend, the latter will easily agree with what he has said.
But he who must feel he has not communicated individual
value, seeing the other as different from himself, must not give
in to the pleasure of seeming sympathy but must still see in the
other the *persona* who denies, suffers, has not, the *persona* he
feels in himself; and respecting in him this *persona,* he must
deny seeming value and bring distant things nearer, making
even more distant things live in the present. Because *to him this
man* must be the entire *world.* And he must be sufficient to the
hunger of the world, not to the *flavor* of that man.

And if he is alone, the world must be a man who always
says no to every one of his actions, every word, until he has
filled by himself the desert and lit up the obscurity.

And if men do not want to understand him, he must not
say, "They're blind, I've given everything already"—he has given
nothing until he has given the proximity of distant things such

---

*Read: until he is "discontent."

that even the blind should see them. He must feel the insufficiency in himself and respect in them that which they do not respect in themselves; so that, attracted by his love, they should take on the *persona* he loves in them: then will the blind see.

Thus must he give in order to have the reason of self and have it in himself in order to give it. Forging the hard path without rest, he must *cultivate individual value in the living, and, making his own life always richer in negations, create himself and the world.*

This is wanting to have things—both oneself in things and in things oneself: for the world is nothing but *my* world, and *if I possess it I have myself.* "React against the need of affirming illusory individuality; have the honesty to deny your own violence, the courage to live the whole pain of your insufficiency at any point—in order to succeed in affirming the person with reason in himself, in order to communicate *individual value:* and be *wholly persuaded, you and the world.*" This is what the Oracle of Delphi said when it said, Γνῶθι σεαυτόν, 'know thyself.'*

## i. Pain Speaks

So the *blind and mute pain* of all the things that, in wanting to be, are not, *will be farsighted and eloquent for the one* who has

---

*Ἐδιζησάμην ἐμεωυτόν, 'I searched into myself' (Heraclitus). [Diels 101.—Translators' note.]

Δίζημαι = I search for a thing I do not know, I search for a thing and at the same time I search to find what this thing is (root ζη < ζητέω > doubled), like one who does not know what a surface closed by a curved line is—but knows it has no angles and knows what angles are—who tries to have it, researching for it among the other figures, discarding all those with angles: *to search by means of negative givens.* So is the search for reason, for the value we do not know, knowing only that *it must not be in regard to the irrationality of need.*

taken on its *persona*, for in gray pleasure, in the finite pains of
all things that, for fear of death, always repress it, he will hear
it speak and see it παπταίνειν, 'watch in anticipation,' a good
that those things do not have the courage to want. He will see
that what men suffer for is not hunger, thirst, disease, or mis-
fortune. Nor are food, drink, apparent health, what is in their
hand but is not theirs (for they do not possess its power) what
can make them content. He will see that obtuse pain suffers in
them in every present, equally empty in abundance or privation. He will suffer at one and the same point of his deficiency
and theirs: speaking the voice of his own pain, he will speak to
them *the distant* voice *of their own pain.* Just as in his intense
activity he will be close to satiating his own pain, so he will
place near them a *life* by which they will see the weave of what
presses and distracts them gradually unravel; they will find
themselves being stable without the fear of instability; they
will see the walls of the tiny room of their misery torn asunder
at a stroke and their tiny light grow dim when he appears like
the dawn of a new day and the outside darkness is no longer
there to press them with its terror. Freed from what they believe indispensable, from cares, from the weight of the myriad
little things in which their life always dissipates and around
which it always turns, from all the misery of their pettiness,
they will taste the joy of a fuller present in the impossible, the
unbearable. They will see that there is nothing to fear, nothing
to seek, nothing to flee from—hunger is not hunger, bread is
not bread; for they will experience their hunger in another
manner, and other bread will have been offered to them. No
longer will they feel cold or fatigue, pains here and desires
there; nor will they be frustrated by need but will feel their life
gathered in the present, for at one point they will have been
made participants in a vaster and deeper life.

To a fragile vessel in the midst of a storm a great ship is a safe port.

In their heavy flight, with each raising of the wing, crows lower their bodies, and no more does the body raise the wings than do the wings lower the body; but in the onrush of the hawk's flight, its body stable, it flaps its wings evenly, raising itself securely upward.

Thus does the man on the path of persuasion maintain at each point the equilibrium of his *persona;* he does not writhe about, he has no uncertainties or moments of fatigue if he never fears pain but has honestly taken on its *persona. He lives it at every point.* And because this pain is common to all things, things live in him not as the correlative of few relations but with vastness and profundity of relations.

Where there is obscurity for others there is light for him, for the circle of his horizon is wider. Where there is mystery and impotence for others, he has power and sees clearly. Because he has the honesty of feeling always insufficient in the face of *infinita potestas,* 'unlimited power,' he makes himself ever more sufficient to things, *sufficing* ever more deeply to the eternal deficiency of things. In him, as in an individual nucleus, ever vaster and more numerous determinations organize themselves.[50] At each point in the presentness of his affirmation *there is the proximity of more distant things.*\*

For this reason, in his presence, his acts, his words, a life transcending the myopia of men reveals itself, "ennucleates" itself, makes itself near, concrete: for this reason Christ has a halo, stones become loaves of bread, the sick are healed, the cowardly become martyrs, and men cry miracle.[51]

---

\*Parmenides 90: λεῦσσε δ᾽ ὅμως ἀπεόντα νόῳ παρεόντα βεβαίως, 'he contemplates distant things with a mind securely near.' [Mullach 90; Diels 4:1.—Translators' note.]

For this reason his every word is luminous because, one being linked to another in a profundity of connections, it creates the presence of what is distant. He can give distant things in proximate appearances so that even he who lives only on the latter finds in them a sense he did not know,* and he can move the heart of everyone.

> Beredt wird einer nicht
> durch fremder Reden Macht,
> ist nicht sein eigen Geist
> zur Redlichkeit gebracht.†

> One does not become eloquent
> through the power of others' words
> if one's own spirit
> is not inclined to honesty.[52]

The just man is good at every thing; he who is unjust to no thing can do every thing.‡

## ii. Pain Is Joy

What he knows, which is the flavor of his vaster life, is the *pleasure* of the moment in every present. His maturity at every point is all the more flavorful as the strength of his pain is sour. Alone in the desert, he lives a dizzying vastness and profundity of life. Whereas philopsychia, ever anxious for the future, ac-

---

*Thus does Christ speak densely and complexly to his disciples and in parables to the people (cf. Matthew 12, I believe). [Matthew 13.—Translators' note.]

†Untranslatable: *redlich* = 'honest,' and *dicibile,* 'speakable.'

‡To be good at one thing means to know how to do it.

celerates time and exchanges one empty present for the next, the stability of the individual preoccupies infinite time in presentness and arrests time. Each of his instants is a century in the life of others—until he *makes of himself a flame* and comes to consist in the final present.[53] Then he will be persuaded and in persuasion have peace.

Δι᾿ ἐνεργείας ἐς ἀργίαν

Through activity to peace.[54]

# II
# On Rhetoric

# I
# Rhetoric

TRANSLATORS' NOTE: *Rhetoric, as contrasted with persuasion, refers to all methods by which humans conceal their true condition from themselves and each other. It is, says Michelstaedter, "the inadequate affirmation of individuality" because "they let themselves sink into words that only feign communication." The classical identification of the aim of rhetoric as persuasion, which is canonical in the tradition that runs from Plato and Aristotle to Cicero and Quintilian, is implicitly rejected, as is the classical contrast between rhetoric and philosophy. What comes to be called philosophy, which is not true wisdom or even the love of it, is for Michelstaedter an example of rhetoric.*

*It is also here that Michelstaedter develops a curious and admittedly original definition of the absolute, a theme first advanced in Part One, Chapter III: the inability of people to live without illusions because of philospychia and fear of death. The person who transcends this has, in Hegel's words, absolute knowledge, though this is not for Michelstaedter the kind of intellectualist knowledge Hegel imagined it to be. Throughout the present chapter Michel-*

*staedter suggests that the belief in the immortal soul keeps people*
*from having to acquire the absolute; they can just defer the problem*
*to another life out of a disguised form of philopsychia.* Here, as in
Nietzsche, is the notion of Christianity as a slave religion.

Michelstaedter's disdain for Cartesian distinctions, which he
approaches as moral and ethical divisions, evident even in his previous comments, is made explicit in his riff on Descartes' argument
Cogito ergo sum. *First, Michelstaedter puts a voluntarist spin on the*
*argument:* "Cogito *means I seek to know, that is, I lack knowledge; I*
do not know." *The sense seems to be that "I think therefore I am" is*
*valid only for the person who does not surrender any sense of his own*
*existence to recognition by others. This is justified by a reference to*
*Parmenides' argument that "it is necessary either to be absolutely or*
*not at all," because any proposition that includes a lack, or negation,*
*is equivalent to a failure to affirm the existence of the referent as "full*
*of existence." The usual range of Descartes' argument, which applies*
*to every person at the moment he or she is reflecting, is relegated to*
*the sphere of rhetoric, that is, trying to persuade oneself that one ex-*
*ists. Knowledge of the reflexive kind prized by Descartes is rhetorical*
*persuasion, not, as it purports to be, true persuasion.*

*Finally, in his "historical example" Michelstaedter presents*
*Socrates as a case study of a person who meets the criteria of being*
*persuaded. The vehicle of the air balloon is an allusion to the pres-*
*entation of Socrates in Aristophanes'* The Clouds. *This is subse-*
*quently run together with an allusion to the perspective offered by*
*the Ideas in Plato's* Republic *and with a set of allusions that link*
*Plato's disciples with those of Jesus. The material on which Michel-*
*staedter builds his account of the reaction of Plato's followers, and*
*Plato's dialogue with them, is made up out of whole cloth. There are*
*no ancient sources for it, as Michelstaedter admits in a note. Aristo-*
*tle is viewed as appropriating the transcendental goods of Socrates,*

*which, the author implies, were more or less well preserved by Plato. This is a crucial transition in the argument: Aristotle intellectualizes the goods lived by Socrates and witnessed by Plato, turning them into a knowledge-acquiring enterprise, something of a knowledge factory. Aristotle stands in here for Hegel and, closer to home, Croce. By extension, we must also think of Michelstaedter as seeing in Aristotle's* Rhetoric *a false view of that subject as something that can be known in the manner of a catalogue.*

Ἠγάπησαν γὰρ τὴν δόξαν τῶν ἀνθρώπων μᾶλλον
ἤπερ τὴν δόξαν τοῦ θεοῦ.

Because they love the glory of men
more than the glory of God.
—St. John[55]

But men grow tired on this path, feeling faint in solitude:[56] the voice of pain is too strong. They no longer know how to endure it with their whole *persona*. They look behind, they look all around, and ask for a blindfold: *they ask to be for someone,* for something. For in the face of the demand for possession they feel insufficient. They want to be a *sufficient persona* for someone or something, with whatever their activity, so that they might repeat the relation in the future, so that the correlate might be certain for them ahead. Their power pretends to be finite, and finite the possession they wanted, their will being persuaded in whatever repeated present moment.

Facing whatsoever limited, finite relation, they do not live it as a simple correlation but pretend to be men with persuasion; beneath the elementary relation that defeats them through their fear of death, they feign a correlative to the persuasion they pretend to have, a stable value that does not become exhausted in the turning of particular relations but remains beneath, fixed, immutable. Because of their philopsychia they need to attribute value to things in the very act of seeking them and at the same time *need* to say their life is not in those things but *is free in persuasion and outside such needs.* Thus do they not confess that the value of these things lies in regard to their finite need; but there, deep down, is the *absolute* value in which they affirm themselves as absolute.

They are still things among things, slaves of this and that, before, after, if, and maybe, in the sway of their needs, fearful of the future, enemies of every other will, unjust toward any other's demand. They still affirm at every point their inadequate *persona.* But this is all appearance; it is not their *persona.* Deep down their absolute *persona* remains, affirming itself absolutely in absolute value, *having absolute value:* finite knowledge. The man stops and says, *I know.*[57]

That man does not live things as any other consciousness does, more or less, affirming itself in every present. For he "also" knows what those things are in themselves: he eats, drinks, sleeps, has weight, walks, falls, gets back up, ages; but his person is not in knowing how to eat, drink, sleep, have weight, or walk more or less well; it is not the *persona* that ages: he "also" knows all these things. And through his knowing he is outside time, space, continual necessity; he is free: *absolute.* He lives on what is given him, of which he does not have reason in himself, but in his absolute knowledge he has Reason; if the end of his life affirmations shows fear of death at every point, in his Ab-

solute he has the End; if he is in the sway of things and has
nothing, and if moreover he defends as valuable this nothing
with injustice toward all other things, in the Absolute he has
Freedom, Possession, Justice. Thus does he carry the Absolute
with him on the streets of the city. He is no longer one but *two:*
a body, matter, or phenomenon, I don't know, and a soul,
form, or idea. And whereas the body lives in the nether world
of matter, time, space, necessity, a slave, the soul lives free in the
absolute.

But if we want to call the stone that falls on my head
body, then my pain is body, my fear of new stones is body,
my power is body, as are the powers that transcend my own:
chance is body and its firstborn son—God—is body. But is
God soul? Then the father too is soul, soul the flowing of powers, soul my power, my fear, my pain, the head, the stone. If I
knew what body meant and what soul meant, I would take one
side bravely,[58] but I don't know. Whether bread is body or soul,
I eat it when hungry, and my stomach, whether body or soul,
satiates itself. Food is good or bad, but taste—I don't know
whether it is body or soul, matter or form. A *persona* has worth,
I take pleasure in speaking with him, love him, but this *persona,*
value, pleasure, love, *I don't know* whether it is body or soul.

What I know is that if the absolute inhabits the soul, it is
sorely pressed because either we start from below and overbearing matter flushes the soul out from the very last recesses
of consciousness, or we start from the top and then the soul itself gives refuge to so many things that they end up driving
away the absolute altogether. How do I know the absolute if I
don't even know the body, you ask? The absolute—I've never
known it, but I know it in the way the man suffering from in-
somnia knows sleep, or the man watching the darkness knows
light. What I know is that my consciousness, whether corpo-

real or soulful, is made of deficiency, *that I do not have the Absolute until I am absolute, that I do not have Justice until I am just, that I do not have Freedom, Possession, Reason, the End, until I am free and finite in myself, lacking nothing that would present itself as an end in the future, but I have a reasonable end here, now, all in the present. I do not wait, search, fear, and I am persuaded.*

But men no longer have need of being persuaded, for from the time they are born, in whatsoever thing they do or say, they have the privilege of an immortal soul, which accompanies them from the arms of their wetnurse, from their first steps and tumbles, through the whole sad turning of their anxiety, pain, fear, through all their illusions and disillusionments, transitions, accommodations, until their deathbed. And in the teary, pleading gaze that asks the doctor for continuation on earth and the priest for continuation beyond the grave, where the fear of death flickers for the last time, there is the immortal soul, with everything in itself, knowing everything. Or if not the soul, which for some is an old-fashioned word, then "spirit," "reason," or simply "thought"—which act in its place and through which man always, even in impotent distress, participates in the absolute: man "*knows*," which is why he is always two: his *life* and his *knowing*.

But how does this knowing affirm itself alongside the life that at every point affirms itself?

When man says, "this is," he directly affirms his own *persona*, his own reality (direct mode).*

When man says, "I know this is," he affirms *himself* in the face of his own reality (connective mode).

---

*See App. I. [The appendices are not included in this edition. —Translators' note.]

In the first case he *wants* something, he affirms the mode, the *persona* of his will. At the point where he places a real thing outside himself, he expresses the flavor that things have for him, his consciousness, his knowing—whichever it may be. In his illusion he says that what "*is for him*" simply "*is*"; he calls it good or bad insofar as it pleases or displeases him.

When man says, "I know this is," he "wants himself wanting"; he again affirms his *persona* in the face of an element of reality that is nothing but the affirmation of his very *persona*. He places his *persona* as real outside of himself in any affirmation.

But if his *persona* were real, had reason in itself, the thing it affirms would be, as its correlative, real and absolute just as it is (ἐὸν γὰρ ἐόντι πελάζει, 'being indeed adheres to being,' Parmenides);[59] it *would be affirmed in itself*. But because he *needs to reaffirm it* with the affirmation of his knowing, he presents it as *not real in itself*—and presents his own *persona*, its correlate, as insufficient.

Now with the reaffirmation of his insufficient *persona* he presumes to attribute value to this thing, which, being for him, is not. But whereas the direct affirmation that lives things, as it lives them, attributes value to them relative to the *persona*—it knows them inasmuch as it wants them—the reaffirmation of this *persona adds nothing to reality*. The former is sufficient to the relativity of what it lives; the latter, which wants to make this relativity absolute, is altogether insufficient, outside life, outside its power: it is *impotent*. The former knows whether a thing is good or bad for its *persona*; the latter knows nothing any longer except that it wants to know: to be a finite *persona*.

For himself a man knows or does not know; but he says he knows for others. His knowing is in life, for the sake of life, but when he says, "I know," "he tells others he is alive," in order to have from others something not given to him for his living affirmation. He wants "to constitute a *persona*" for himself with the affirmation of the absolute *persona* he does not have: *it is the inadequate affirmation of individuality: rhetoric.*\* Men speak always and call their speaking reasoning. But ὁποῖα ἄν τίς ποτε λέγῃ οὐδὲν λέγει ἀλλ᾽ ἀπολογεῖται, 'no matter what one says, one says nothing, only justifies himself'; no matter what someone says, he is not saying but attributing voice to himself for speaking, flattering himself.

Just as a child cries out in the dark to make a sign of its own *persona*, which, in its infinite fear, it senses is insufficient, so men, who in the solitude of their empty spirit feel insufficient, inadequately affirm themselves, feigning the sign of the *persona* they do not have, "knowledge," as if it were already in their hands. They no longer hear the voice of things telling them, "You are," and amidst the obscurity they do not have the *courage* to endure, but each seeks his companion's hand and says, "I am, you are, we are," so that the other might act the mirror and tell him, "you are, I am, we are"; and together they repeat, "we are, we are, because we know, because we can tell each other the words of knowledge, of free and absolute consciousness." *Thus do they stupefy one another.*†

Having nothing and able to give nothing, they let themselves sink into words that feign communication, because none of them can make his world be the world of the others;

---

\*Life is an irrational value in every consciousness (ἄλογος κατὰ φύσιν, 'irrational by nature,' Heraclitus) [Mullach 76; not attested by Diels, but compare Diels A, 16, 148:35.—Translators' note], an implicit error of logic— but rhetoric has twice the irrational factor of illusion. Thus does Christ say, τυφλοὶ ἦτε ὅτι μὴ βλέπετε ἀλλὰ λέγετε ὅτι βλέπομεν, ἁμαρτία ὑμῶν μένει, 'To the degree that you did not see you would be blind; but you say, "We see," your sin remains.' [John 9:41.—Translators' note.]

†For the same inadequate affirmation men take pleasure in singing or reciting other people's things.

they feign words containing the absolute world, and with words they nourish their boredom, making for themselves a poultice for the pain; with words they show what they do not know and what they need in order to soothe the pain or make themselves numb to it. Each word contains mystery, and they entrust themselves to words, weaving with them thereby a new, tacitly agreed-upon veil over the obscurity: καλλωπίσματα ὄρφνης, 'ornaments of the darkness': "God help me"—because I haven't the courage to help myself.

They need "knowledge," and knowledge is formed. "Knowledge" in and of itself becomes the goal of life. There are parts of knowledge, a way to knowledge, men who seek it, men who give it, it is bought, sold, for this much, in that much time, with that much effort. Thus *rhetoric flourishes alongside life.* Men put themselves into a *cognitive attitude and make knowledge.*

But because knowledge is needed in this manner, it is also necessary that there be demand. Otherwise the men who know, for whom would they know? What would a nurse be if there were no sick? And what a strange animal would a doctor be then! But the sick are created. When youngsters beat their wings to rise above ordinary life, when the call of life springs from their hearts, strange and incomprehensible even to them, when they demand to be truly men, this is none other than "*thirst for knowledge,*" one says, and with the water of knowledge their flame is extinguished. The certain end, the reason for being, freedom, justice, possession, everything is given them in finite *words* applied to diverse things and then extracted from those things. If they ask for life in each thing, for each the response "to this curiosity" of theirs is ὄνομα ἐπίσημον, 'the name as conventional sign' (Parmenides).[60] Then rhetoric engulfs like the current of a swollen river on whose bank you cannot maintain your footing without getting swept into the middle. "Give the devil an inch and he takes a mile," the saying goes. Indeed, *getting used to a word is like acquiring a vice.*

"Curiosity that demands the name," said one elegant philosopher, "is the first sign of philosophical virtue." Indeed! How well he defined "philosophy"—better than he knew.

In fact, the first sign of renunciation in taking possession of things for "love of knowledge" is when one contents oneself with the conventional sign that hides the distinctly intangible obscurity, presuming in this sign, through this convention, to have *knowledge,* each time a little scrap of knowledge that, linked and subordinated to other scraps through various and admirable concatenations of philosophical curiosity, forms a system of names and *constitutes* for him *the inviolable possession of absolute knowledge.*

In this well-engineered brain of his, he is free and absolute master, able to descend from the most general and abstract to the most particular and close, and with no less ease, to climb up from the latter to the former, able to give a name for a thing upon request and for this name, by ascending or descending along the way of likenesses or definitions, feign a vast ray of light.

The system of names covers the room of individual misery with mirrors, through which a thousand times and ever infinitely ahead the same light of the same things in infinite ways is *reflected.*

If hunger remains unsatisfied, if time removes every good from every present, if pain continues, mute, ungraspable, if the darkness outside presses ever more—what does it matter? We *are reflecting:* we are in the freedom of thought when we apply its forms to things: *cogitamus ergo sumus,* 'we think; therefore, we are.' The rest are trifles of individual life: for thought there is no deficiency, no obscurity: in the system of knowledge lives *the absolute freedom of the spirit.*

Oh the vanity, fenced in by dense oaks!

But *cogito* does not mean "I know"; *cogito* means I seek to know: that is, I lack knowledge: *I do not know.* Wanting a thing to men is having it, wanting to know is knowing, being on the way of knowledge, having in oneself the finite means and manners for knowledge. If they knew already, they would move no more, no longer having the need of self-affirmation; if they had no way to get to knowledge, they also would not move because they would have no way to do so: *We know or do not know:* ἢ πάμπαν πελέμεν χρεών ἐστιν ἢ οὐκί, 'it is necessary either to be absolutely or not to be at all' (Parmenides).[61] But men's necessity is in fact *moving:* not white, not black, but gray. They are and are not, they know and do not know: *thought becomes.* Givens in themselves are nothing, men say: we must now grasp them, consider them *sub specie aeterni*, contemplate them, and *in thinking* go toward knowledge. *Value, reality* is the way, the machine that moves concepts, *philosophical activity.*

But if thinking means to *agitate concepts*, which *merely by this activity* must *become knowledge*, I am always empty in the present, and the care of the future wherein I feign my goal *deprives me of my entire being. Cogito = non-entia coagito, ergo non sum,* 'I think = I agitate non-entities; therefore, I am not.'

This is the life rhetoric feigns for the man alongside life, the life of the thing they call *intellect*, which if it really were, would stop living. It is the noblest, highest life, the only virtuous life, that which lifts us out of human miseries as well as *the duty of being men* in this mortal world, because by means of this life we participate in *divinity.* You adapt yourself to the system, concepts, modes; you enter into the method of classifications, definitions, or the more refined method of outdoing,[62] and you *work*. Through this work given to you, knowing and not knowing on the paths beaten by others, you will know, or others will know because of your effort.

But you do nothing, know nothing, say nothing, even if the way on which you believe yourself to be is that of the wisest man on earth. And if you rely on him and burden him with what weighs you down, you always remain invalid. His words, in which you make for yourself an absolute value, are your choice, of which *you comprehend what you can grasp*. There is nothing made, nor any way prepared, nor finite manner or work, through which you can attain life, nor any words that can give you life, because life lies precisely in creating everything by yourself, in not adapting yourself to any path. There is no language, you must create it; you must create the manner, you must create each thing, in order to have your life for yourself. The first Christians made the sign of the fish and believed themselves saved. If they had only made more fish, they would have been truly saved because by so doing they would have recognized that Christ saved himself,* because out of his mortal life he was able to create god, the individual; they would have seen that no one is saved by him unless he follows his own life. But to follow does not mean *imitating*, placing oneself with whatever value one has amid the manners and words of the way of persuasion, with the hope of having truth in that value. *Si duo idem faciunt non est idem*, 'if two people do the same thing, it is not the same thing.'[64] The sense of one's activity is not what the near sight sees of what one has done, but

*Ἰησοῦς Χριστὸς Θεοῦ Ὑὸς Σωτήρ. / Ἰησοῦς Χριστὸς Θεοῦ Ὑὸς Ἑαυτοῦ Σωτήρ, 'Jesus Christ God's Savior Son. / Jesus Christ God's Son Savior of Himself.'[63]

the *mind* with which one has done it, which only with *equal mind*[65] can be relived and re-cognized *in the tiniest sign*. But for the myopic, that sign is only a sign hiding the obscurities that transcend it. About the living organism he knows what an ant knows with regard to a man's body when it walks about that body's unknown plains and depressions. He who contents himself with such signs, and out of the repetition of the proximity he knows makes himself a sufficient labor, is not saved but lost. His labor is to him a dark torment, a brute exertion, which for him does not have reason in itself at the moment he does it but is, *for having done it*, for the distant hope. "The labor of the fool wearies him—for he does not know the way to the city" (Ecclestiastes).[66]

The path of persuasion is not traversed by "omnibuses"; it has no signs or indications that one can communicate, study, repeat. But each has in himself the need to find it and in his own pain the indicator; each must open his way by himself, for each is alone and can hope for no help except from himself. The way of persuasion has nothing but this indication: do not adapt yourself to the sufficiency of what is given to you. The few who have traversed it with honesty have found themselves at the same point, and to him who understands them they appear, in different ways, on the same luminous path. The way to health cannot be seen except by healthy eyes ὅσον τ᾽ ἐπὶ θυμὸς ἱκάνοι, 'and only as far as the spirit may reach' (Parmenides).[67]

You who seek prudence, knowledge, absolute affirmation, you who seek the peace of knowledge, the sharpness of the gaze, you who seek pleasure—pleasure is the flower of pain, sweetness the flower of sourness, sharpness the flower of profundity, peace the flower of activity, affirmation the flower of negation, taste the flower of hunger, *prudence the flower of courage;* for

pain seeks not pleasure but possession, profundity not sharpness but life, activity not peace but work, negation not to affirm but to deny, hunger not flavor but bread; *courage not prudence but the act.*

I recite litanies but this changes nothing: what is certain
is that at the point where one *turns to look at one's profile in the
shadow, one destroys it.*[68] Thus, by turning toward *knowing,*
which is the *persona,* the actual consciousness of the honest
will of persuasion, man destroys it forever.

If I were speaking about other pleasures that man—at
the point of seeking them—destroys, everyone would agree but
say this is something else. On the contrary, it is exactly the same:

Οὐδὲ καλᾶς σοφίας ἐστὶν χάρις
εἰ μή τις ἔχει σεμνὰν ὑγίειαν

. . . . .

Τὶς γὰρ ἀδονὰς ἄτερ
θνατῶν βίος ποθεινὸς ἢ ποία τυραννίς,
τᾶς δ' ἄτερ οὐδὲ θεῶν ζαλωτὸς αἰών.

No good comes to us from knowledge
if noble health is absent.

. . . . .

Since without the pleasure that attracts us,
mortal life or tyrranical power,
nothing is worthy of envy, not even the life of a god.

                                                          Simonides

Pleasure is the actuality of my whole *persona* as determinate potency in the present affirmation: food is sweet to me in
the manner and quantity that suits my *persona* (see Part One,
Chapter II, Section i).

When man senses the insufficiency of his *persona* and feels faint before that which escapes his power, he turns to *research* the positions where the actual sense of his *persona* had previously flattered him with the voice of pleasure, "You are," or in the positions that he knows lavish pleasure on others. But at the point where he does this, *he is already outside the healthy turning of his potency,* for he no longer searches for food or a woman or wine as necessary to the continuation of his potency, his health, and in a measure suitable to this, but rather seeks *flavor for flavor's sake.* He seeks what is no longer at the point where he seeks it. Eurydice, whom the infernal gods conceded to Orpheus, was the flower of his song, his *certain* spirit. When on the harsh, obscure path toward life he turned, overcome by anxious care, Eurydice was no longer there.

No matter how much one tries and retries "the pleasures," placing and re-placing himself in the known positions, he will find them *unsuitable,* insipid, or unpleasurable. He has *lost health.* Flavor was the actuality of his *persona,* which wanted to be and in this actuality enjoyed the illusion of individuality. Wanting this as a value in and of itself, he becomes double, looks at himself in the mirror; he wants *to enjoy himself twice over* * and by means of vanity degenerates, becoming ever more vain. Pleasure is no longer his pleasure but a *commonplace;* it is "the pleasures." And with respect to these he always affirms himself inadequately, so that he no longer has the criterion but instead it is outside his own potency: it is the *rhetoric of pleasure.*

Thus do impotent artists seek "the impression," placing and re-placing themselves in the known positions, so that as they seek it they do not have it but have only their own will to

---

*I want enjoyment $=$ I want myself wanting (because enjoyment is nothing but the correlative of my will, my person).

have it, and in piteous rhetoric they vainly exploit their organisms, precious with refined sensations.*

In the same manner, the researchers of truth who, for fear of the obscurity, feign for themselves an absolute life in the elaboration of knowing and say, γλυκὺ τὸ γνῶναι, 'sweet is knowing,' are *already overcome by the obscurity:* they are outside life and any health of the organism; they no longer have the sweetness of any knowing. And consuming their betrayal of nature, which wants to attain persuasion in finite Man, they have already betrayed themselves. Their consciousness is no longer a living organism, a presence of things in the presentness of the *persona,* but a *memory,* an inorganic aggregate of names linked to the fictitious organism of the system.†
In this manner, with his rhetoric man not only does not proceed but descends the ladder of organisms and reduces his *persona* to the *inorganic.* He is less alive than any animal. Happy indeed are the beasts with no "immortal soul" that throws them into the chaos of rhetorical impotence, for they maintain themselves in the healthy turning of whatever their potency is.‡

---

*Our own time teaches us that from the very impression of such emptiness one may make art. Whatever I say, since I am an artist and I said it, it is necessarily art.

†Everyone can experience the impotence of memory for recalling any sort of name without a subject that's been lost along the way. Find a tree that forgets how to bloom in the spring! And on the other hand the very presence of a memory alongside the presentness of one's *persona* is a sickness: *an organism does not tolerate foreign bodies.* "To memorize" is translated in German as 'auswendig *lernen*'!

‡And if some say that women have no soul, they speak a truth they are unaware of, because—except for the *neutre,* also a benefit of our time—women do not actually have rhetoric; rather, they are always the same demand for a "man"; and in this they are betrayed by man even before being born.

But the inadequate affirmation of men, who want a know-ing *persona,* has no criterion, no limit, just as the other voices of impotence have neither criterion nor limit: the voice of rage, of precaution, of wine, and of juvenile impertinence, of desperation, where man's *persona,* already overcome by the obscurity, always affirms itself inadequately.

When a man speaks of himself in order to constitute a *persona* for himself and there is no limit or criterion to what he says, whether it be vulgar or strange, petty or great, pleasant or painful, honorable or shameful—because he says it of himself, as proper to him, as made by him—he believes it can con-stitute the *persona* he feels is lacking in him. In the same way, philosophical-literary rhetoric *raves,* as it sets its thought in action with the obscure labor of system and method, thought which *participates* by means of its categories *in the ab-solute.* Such rhetoric always *has said* and *given* what *has ab-solute value* and constitutes for that rhetoric the *persona of absolute knowledge.*

## A Historical Example*

In his love of liberty, Socrates resented being subject to the law of gravity. And he thought the good lay in independence from gravity, because it is this, he thought, that prevents us from ris-ing to the sun.

Being independent from gravity means not having weight, and Socrates did not allow himself rest until he had eliminated all his weight. But having consumed together the hope of freedom and slavery, the independent spirit and grav-

---

*Supporting notes: see App. 2. [The appendices are not included in this edition—Translators' note.]

ity, the necessity of the earth and the will for the sun, he neither flew to the sun nor remained on earth; he was neither independent nor a slave, neither happy nor wretched. But about
him I have nothing more to say.

Plato saw this wondrous end of the master and was dis-
quieted. For he had the same great love, though he was not of
so desperate a devotion. So he concentrated on meditating. He
had to find a μηχάνημα, a 'mechanism,' to raise himself to
the sun, but, deceiving gravity, *without losing weight, body, life.*
He meditated for a long time, and then invented the *macro-
cosm.* The central part of the strange machine was a great, rigid
globe of steel, which with his most affectionate cares for the
high Plato had filled with the *Absolute.* He removed the air
from it, we would say today. With this admirable system he
would rise up without losing his own weight, without lessen-
ing his own life.

The departure was cheered by daring hopes, and the
air balloon rose rapidly upward from the lower strata of the
atmosphere.

"See how we rise up *solely through the will of the absolute,*" Plato exclaimed to his disciples who were with him and
pointed at the shimmering sphere that drew them in its rapid
ascent.

"It is by *its virtue* that we go toward the sun, where gravity no longer rules, and from the bonds of the latter, we free
ourselves little by little."

(Actually we say now that the cause of the balloon's ascent is not "its wanting to rise up" but rather the *falling* of the
air heavier than it.) But Plato exulted in the inebriation of ex-
alting himself and, pointing to the sphere filled with the absolute, he exclaimed: "Behold our soul!"

And the disciples, who did not understand but felt the dizziness and nausea of ascending, watched their teacher, the sphere, and the earth that fled ever lower with dismay.

When they reached the limits of the atmosphere, however, the balloon decreased in speed, wavered, and stopped altogether, balanced in the sea of air. One cannot go beyond the atmosphere: one must content oneself with floating. And hope? The sun? Independence? The disciples watched their teacher with silent request.

So Plato *looked at the lower depths* and ὑπῆρχε αὐτῷ μεγαλοπρέπεια καὶ θεωρία παντὸς μὲν χρόνου πάσης δὲ οὐσίας, 'there opened up for him the magnificent vision of all time and all being';[69] and he was pleased and told the disciples with him: "Here *we are on high;* see below the things of the nether world. They are lower because they are heavy, because they have *weight,* but we," he said, pointing to the sphere that floated immobile above their heads, "we *have 'the lightness,'* we're here only because we have 'the lightness.'"

His disciples leaned over the parapet too, but dismay at the void overcame them so that, pulling back and nearly fainting, they no longer dared to rise from the bottom of the basket. "We," the teacher continued, "*in that we are* here, also *participate in the lightness, and we each have 'the lightness,'* and we each have body and weight but *according to 'the lightness.'*"

"Teacher!" said one of the disciples who had recovered somewhat from the weight of dismay and amazement, "how is the lightness made?"

"The 'lightness,'" began Plato, contemplating the admirable spectacle of things, which to his stronger gaze were as clear as if they'd been nearby, "the 'lightness' contains all things; not as they are with their weight in the world below but without weight; and just as the weight belongs to the body, the 'incorporeal' belongs to the lightness; and if extension, form, color—all that in which men on earth are implicated—belong to the body, to the lightness belongs the unextended, the formless, the colorless, the spiritual. *Merely by the contemplation* of the lightness, we who have the lightness see and possess all things not as they appear on earth but *as they are in the kingdom of the sun.*"

The disciples listened in silence with their gaze intent on the blinding splendor of the steel, and no one wanted to confess not being able to see anything. But from time to time they urged their teacher to say more. And then he talked about the marvels hidden from others, which his sharp gaze discerned, as things on the surface of the earth appeared to him through the vertiginous depth, grouped in various, new, and admirable manners. These new creatures he called ideas, and of them he said they were all closed in the "lightness," and that everybody could see them. The disciples, who saw nothing, abandoned themselves to the suggestiveness of his visions. And if the earth grew dark by night, if the clouds prevented him from seeing, if his eyes grew tired, still he continued in his rapture to narrate, digging from his memory the most remote images and combining them with bizarre fantasies, and he nourished himself and the others with words.

But days, months, years passed. Life did not change. And there was no hope of change. The inhabitants of lightness and Plato himself grew older: indeed, the kingdom of the sun was distant, and the reflected splendor of the machine filled with the absolute, just as it gave neither joy, nor peace, nor freedom, so did it not give eternal youth.

In the absence of any means of salvation, any activity in

which they could be sufficient, the disciples had grown brutish in a dark, desperate torpor. But one day, the one of them most daring and least reverent, having observed that while speaking the teacher kept his eyes always fixed on the distant earth, again leaned over the parapet and saw the void; he strained his gaze in every manner possible to discern something but saw nothing except the shimmering of the waters, like a distant fog, alternating with the dark masses of the earth; and it did not bear the least resemblance to what the teacher was describing. He was not one to *melt* like his companions for fear of the void. Fear matured in him in determinate plans, and in their implementation he displayed an irresistible alacrity. In his jealous heart, moreover, he could hardly stand being blind where his teacher saw clearly, and he made within himself a resolution for finding the means of returning to the earth. From that day he set about studying the ingenious machine that had lifted them up with great attention, and, obtaining the necessary information from his teacher with shrewd questions, soon he had acquired a minute knowledge of all the *mechanisms.*

Coming forward, he spoke to old Plato thus: "Teacher, you say we have the lightness?"

"Otherwise we wouldn't be up here at the very least," said Plato.

"And we are light through the presence of the lightness?"

"Certainly."

"And each thing insofar as it is light is such through the presence of the lightness?"

"Doubtless."

"And conversely the lightness is such as to be able to make everything light through its presence."

"In the same manner."

"Teacher, why could we not take a little of the air around us and put it into the lightness? According to the reasoning about which we have just agreed, it would lose its heavy nature and also participate in the lightness." And he fell silent. Plato looked long into his myopic eyes with his own far-seeing eyes, and he saw that he was being betrayed. But the young disciple knew the mechanism and reasoned soundly, and Plato could not avoid the conclusion. He knew, moreover, how and where he himself had erred. Nor could he, now an old man, deny life to his young disciple.

He lowered his head sadly and said to the youth, "All right. Go ahead!" The disciple busied himself with the valve, and Plato followed his movements melancholically. But for him, too, after all, the vertiginous height, the unbreathable air, the lack of all the dear things of life and of commerce among men, the immobility of all things in the turning of days and nights, carried a sinister sense of void that his words could not fill and that did not differ much from fear. Therefore, when the air began whistling, penetrating impetuously into the sphere, and awakened the poor disciples from their torpor, Plato felt his old heart relax while his ξηρὴ ψυχή, 'dry soul,' grew moist with distant desires.[70]

The balloon descended, the disciples returned to life. "We're going down! We're going down!" They could say nothing but this again and again, which announced the joy they had despaired of finding, the joy of having solid ground under their feet, of being forever outside and safe from that terrible, vertiginous solitude.

And while Plato, despite himself, was intent on observing how the air penetrated into the sphere, they gathered around, animated by change and new hopes and made more curious by the variety of things they were beginning to catch sight of now on the earth's surface, and with greater insistence they asked him to speak again.

And Plato, with both old people's love of storytelling and habit acquired over the years, described what was unfolding before his gaze. But by then there was earthly air inside the balloon's rigid housing, and as the view was lowered, his words no longer seemed pure and suitable to what he had always taught. But what was nearest and most distant preoccupied him, along with the limited and always varied horizon and the varied perspectives of the same things. And, little accustomed to the heavier air, he soon died.

Meanwhile the earth approached, and his disciples' eyes burned with impatience. With natural authority the traitor took his teacher's place, and with the same manners as the latter, as one who knew the mechanism in depth, he began to speak *although he saw nothing distinctly,* but only by means of *acquired habit* and speech said more about the functioning of the mechanism and the behavior of the air amidst the lightness than about what appeared to the sight. When they reached the earth, he began introducing this and that inside the sphere and pronounced the "lightness" of them all. Then he began to observe them in their reciprocal relations, and because he was among them and not above them, going from one to another with his mechanism, he began to θεωρεῖν ὑπὲρ πάσης οὐσίας, 'theorize on all being.' All the people ran to take from him the *goods* that *came from the absolute.* He was a practical spirit and took the goods that were most in fashion, and which lent themselves to the eye, needs, and taste of the public, and placed on them a brand name with the logo "lightness." And the public was happy to be able to say *the goods came from the sky and to use them just as if they'd been goods of this earth.*

That man was Aristotle.*

His system, which at that time had its greatest following, still lives among us, if under different guises, in those who—*repeating, on positive ground, the voice of things as it is given by proximate modes and proximate necessities*—elaborate it *in the name of absolute knowledge* and busy themselves with *theorizing about things.*

---

*It goes without saying that, just as I do not truly claim that Plato was a balloonist, so I do not wish to conjecture on his relations with Aristotle as if these had really taken place. But certainly the last dialogues and especially the *Parmenides* are pervaded by an Aristotelian spirit and seem a prelude to the Categories and the *Metaphysics* of Aristotle. Of the Platonic they have no more than clichés. One can also openly say that they were not made by Plato but by one who had nothing to say and struggled to harmonize the system of ideas with the necessities of a polymorphous speech, as it would later assert itself in Aristotelian works, a tendency that must have been already in the air—or perhaps the author was Plato himself, though a Plato who was old and forgetful, or one of his disciples.

The dissolving of the world of ideas in the infinite weave of forms—of which these dialogues (*Parmenides, The Sophist, The Politician*) mark an intermediate revelatory point—such as it took place then in the philosophical plotting of the idealists is a necessity that, even under other guises, repeats itself whenever men materially follow the way of a better man and busy themselves with concepts without value for them.

# II
# The Constitution
# of Rhetoric

TRANSLATORS' NOTE: *The claim that Aristotle betrayed wisdom by converting it into a collection of all knowledge gives way here to a view of modern science, which purports to see itself as the very opposite of "mere" rhetoric, as the highest example of rhetoric. Just as in Part One, where Michelstaedter dealt first with inanimate things and then animate beings from the perspective of persuasion, so in Part Two he first treats the paradigmatically inanimate objects of science and then animate beings from the perspective of rhetoric. In general terms, this chapter addresses the pretension of modern science to escape the world of rhetoric by becoming objective not only with regard to things but to persons as well, with the rise of social science. "We do not look at things with the eye of hunger or thirst," the scientist protests. "We look at them objectively." Michelstaedter argues that attention to objects is an act of the will and hence cannot be objective in the sense that modern science assumes.*

*In the presentation of the argument we find echoes of the slide between Stoicism and Skepticism, which is the topic on which Hegel builds his treatment of "the merely observing or representational consciousness"—more or less the objectivity pose of science. Stoics hold that thinking is an act of the will. Hence they admit the very premise that Michelstaedter taxes modern science with forgetting. But then, because will is personal rather than objective, a skeptical moment sets in, as in Hegel. This, then, appears to be a rewriting of Chapter 30 of Hegel's* Phenomenology of Mind *from a purely voluntarist perspective.*

*Μηδέ σ᾽ ἔθος πολύπειρον ὁδὸν κατὰ τήνδε βιάσθω.*

*Nor should clever habit push you along this road.*

—Parmenides[71]

i

"Whereas philosophy has raved through metaphysical exaltation, we have placed it once more on positive ground; and here, maintaining our contact with reality, we have a secure means of conquering truth."

In this manner, more or less, through the mouths of its lovers, that which gradually supplants the old mother speaks: *modern science*. It would be enough to ask what difference there is between reality and truth, because of which, while being in contact with reality, one must still forge a path to attain truth. But modern science

has so many legs
that it's no wonder if it takes
more effort than usual to knock them out.

So if I were talking with a scientist and said to him, "If you have reality, what are you still fussing about? Or if you do not have it, because with your work you (who don't have it) do not add anything to it, μάλ᾽ αὖθις, 'all the more,' why all the fuss? Do we know or not? If we know, we are like so many Gods in eternal peace; if we do not, *gloria in excelsis deo et pax* (peace at least) *hominibus in terra*, 'Glory to god in the highest, and peace to men on earth.'"

Οὕτως ἢ πάμπαν πελέμεν χρεών ἐστιν ἢ οὐκί.

Thus it is necessary either to be absolutely or not to be at all.

—(Parmenides)[72]

"Μάλ᾽ ἀπαίδευτος εἶ," 'You are truly uncultured,' he would answer, ὑπόδρα ἰδών, 'looking askance.' "This dilemma itself is a metaphysical vanity. Reality is reality and thought is thought. When one puts his teeth in contact with an apple, one must busy one's jaw in order to eat it. So it is with reality. Every instant of life man comes into contact with a part of reality, and each man in his life has come into contact with only one part; each age, generation, century, civilization comes into contact with just one; millennia will pass, and it will never be whole. . . . What does 'Do we know or not' mean? We know one part today, tomorrow another, in all the days of our life we know ever other parts. Thus I acquire knowledge for my part; thus every other son of man acquires it for his part each day of his life beneath the sky, and we pass on to our descendents the inheritance of our knowledge, so that they should acquire more, and it should always add ever more truths, and the body of human science should be constituted. Now, to be able to pass on his share, not only that, but to be able to retain it for himself, each man must bind it in its fragments σὺν αἰτίας λο-γισμῷ, 'with consideration for the cause.' *You must make a treasure of the experience.*"

Here again is preconception, *anticipatio,* in the αἰτία, 'cause' and the λογισμός, 'consideration'; what is the αἰτία, what the possible λογισμός of him who does not yet have the truth but must await the flight of millennia in order to have it? Or if he has αἰτία, what need does he have still to worry about reality? What is the satiety of the man who has not eaten, and what is the necessity of eating to the man who is satiated? But this might seem a desire δυσχεραίνειν ἐν τοῖς λόγοις, 'to quibble with words': for here reason has only the function of holding steady this "*experience.*" And one may very well be curious to know what that thing actually might be. "Open your eyes, your ears, your nostrils," any scientist will answer me. "Use your tongue and hands and you'll have the healthy and positive experience of the senses."

But this experience, in my own experience, is quite a strange experience.

What is the taste of bread? That of the first piece I eat when I am hungry or the one I eat after, when I am full? What is the smell of roast? The good, dear aroma that overpowers all other smells and wafts about me as I search in vain for food, or that of the piece left over on my table? And the eye, what does the eye see? I truly believe that everyone can experience the dubious sight of one's eye and be uncertain as to the faces of those closest to him.

Look at the face of a friend you trust and you find a noble visage. You locate the nobility either in the nose or the fore-head or "a certain something of the eyes"; look at him when he has betrayed you and you see a vile mouth, a sinister glance, "an expression that's just not right." (And if one looks at a woman before and after one has had one's way with her, the contradiction strikes even more stridently). What is the experience of reality?

If I am hungry, reality is nothing more to me than an ensemble of more or less edible things. If I am thirsty, reality is more or less liquid, and more or less potable. If I am sleepy, it is a great bed more or less hard. If I am not hungry, not thirsty, not sleepy, and do not need any other determinate thing, the world is a large ensemble of grays that are I don't know what but that certainly are not made to cheer me up.

## ii

"But we do not look at things with the eye of hunger or thirst," the scientist protests. "We look at them *objectively.*"

"Objectivity" too is a pretty word.

To see things as they are, not because one needs them, but in themselves: to have at one point "ice and the rose, great cold and great warmth almost in a single moment,"[73] all things in the actuality of my life, "Only the whole of eternity assembled . . ."[74]

Is this objectivity?

On paper you can address such a question to whomever you want, but if you addressed it aloud to a scientist, you would not come out in one piece. With this question, in fact, you would risk having all knowledge again in the present or not having it at all; and your dear hope, your absolute, your God, your work, would be destroyed.

And yet if "objectivity" means "objectivity," to see objectively either has no sense because it must have a *subject* or it is the extreme consciousness of the man who is *one with things, has* all things in himself: ἒν συνεχές, 'one, indivisible,' the persuaded: god.

The "consciousness of things for themselves and not for my need" must necessarily be all *in one present;* and this present must be the last present because otherwise things would not be for themselves but for the sake of continuing for some need. Therefore, the *objectivity* of scientific work in which the men of science flourish, κῆρα δὲ τότε δέξονται, 'except for yielding to death,'

όππότε κεν δὴ
Ζεὺς ἐθέλη τελέσαι ἠδ᾽ ἀθάνατοι θεοὶ ἄλλοι

when Jove or the other
immortal gods decide to mark the end,[75]

cannot be that catastrophic objectivity because otherwise their experimenting would be a self-affirmation similar to that of the bee that dies stinging, and the first experiment, the baptism of science, would be the baptism of death.

"But we don't see," the men of science again protest. "We watch *objectively.*" Watch is also a verb, and as such it wants a subject. And because scientists cannot discard their skin with impunity like silkworms in order to watch how things are made, we must admit that *objectivity* is τρόπον τινά, 'in some manner,' a *subjectivity.* Then we must go to the other extreme: if it is not god, it is stone. If it is not the identity of my consciousness with the consciousness of things, *it is the infinitesimal consciousness of the infinitesimal relation,* and in this lies the illusion of absence of every *individual assent;** for assent

*I use "assent" to say "presentness of the *persona* in the present affirmation." *Adsensus:* thus Cicero translates the συγκατάθεσις of Zeno the Stoic, *Acad. pr.* II 144: *"cum extensis digitis adversam manum ostenderat 'visum' (δόξα) inquiebat 'huiusmodi est.' Deinde cum paullum digitos contraxerat 'adsensus huiusmodi,'"* 'Holding out his palm with his fingers out-

cannot be taken away altogether. In order to have *objective ex-perience I must watch the things I do not see,* for those that I see, I see by the assent of my entire *persona.*

And *to watch* means to procure for the eye the proximity that reawakens *its assent,* not as eye that serves my body but as *eye,* as *ensemble of lenses, inorganic assent.*

I see another crowd of people on this very way leading to inorganic assent. And I know the dignified ranks of scientists could hardly stand being close to them—if they noticed. But eyes preoccupied with watching do not see.

This is the crowd of revelers, who seek pleasure for plea-sure's sake and at the point they seek it no longer have it (see Part Two, Chapter I), for their *persona* dissolves. If the mouth no longer takes pleasure in what it knows is good for the body but wants to repeat this pleasure even though it may be detri-mental to the body, then it is no longer my mouth but *a mouth that wants to live for itself.* But even if it re-searches and multi-plies the things that once gave it pleasure in the service of the body, now it does not manage to draw out the sweet flavor; that sweetness belonged to the body and to its continuation, and the mouth suffers the bitter disappointment that bread and meat have become flavorless to it. It seeks the sweet for its own sake and the salty and the spicy, and man thereby pro-cures for the chemical determinations of his own organ the proximity of the things necessary to their affirmation, and he assumes the *persona* of that nearly atomlike life. The same oc-curs for all other senses in the degeneration of pleasure.* The

---

stretched, he maintained, "Such is representation made." Then, curving his fingers slightly: "Such is assent." Joh. v. Arnim, *Stoicorum veterum Frag-menta,* vol. I, Lipsiae, 1905.

*Perhaps in order to signify this self-dissolving, this loss of solidity or "pouring out" of the person, the Romans said "*liquida voluptas.*"

same occurs in the re-search of knowledge for knowledge's sake, for one arrives at the knowledge of the organs for their own sake and not as organs of my person, and *one re-searches the flavor of the world with regard to inorganic assent.*\*

Try looking at the things you do not see, and you will see lines, bodies, colors. What they are you will not know because you have not seen them: the eye does not know by itself, the lens does not know. The eye knows what it knows only *in that it is your eye.* Set yourself the task, for example, of watching *objectively* the face of the friend in which you now see "a vile mouth and an expression out of place," and try to retrieve the nobility of the nose and forehead you used to love: you find lines and angles and curves and protrusions of a given form but about which you can say nothing; the word "noble" said of noses and foreheads is devoid of meaning, the nose and noble forehead indifferent and incomprehensible.

Or take for instance a *point.* We all know the point pricks, but in vain would I want to reduce this knowledge to an objective experience: the eye would see a punctual form sticking in a hand and drops of blood, and the hand would feel an unpleasant impression, *but I would not know the point pricks,* for the eye must not be my eye and the hand not my hand if I really want to be *objective.* And the simultaneity of the two experiences must be chance for the objective observer, and he must especially avoid establishing it as a rule: only after repeated vigorous experiments could he hazard the hypothesis that perhaps the two things might have a certain "causal link."

I happened to see some children amusing themselves (very philosophically) with cards painted with overlapping red and blue figures. By looking through red and blue pieces of

---

\*The organ is organ only in that it is an organ of the organism.

glass, which from time to time eliminated the figures of the same color, they managed to reproduce the resulting others in drawings.

But one of them kept to himself and, having thrown the colored pieces of glass spitefully away, was intent on copying with tenacious care, line by line, the tangle of overlapping figures.

There, I thought, that one will be a scientist: he is already sacrificing his play to objectivity, and watches and copies what he has not seen, what has no *meaning* for him.

Indeed, scientists in their experiments experience the blindness of the eyes, the deafness of the ears, the obtuseness of each of their senses. In vain did Parmenides offer the admonishment,

> Μηδέ σ᾽ ἔθος πολύπειρον ὁδὸν κατὰ τήνδε
> βιάσθω
> νωμᾶν ἄσκοπον ὄμμα καὶ ἠχήεσσαν ἀκουὴν καὶ
> γλῶσσαν.

> Nor should clever habit push you along this road,
>     so that you are guided by the eye without light,
>     the deafened ear, and the tongue.[76]

In order to render this obtuse, autonomous life of the senses more *intense*, science multiplies their potency with ingenious equipment. But this intensification is none other than the repetition of the same proximity, the broadening of the same determination. Just as when you take hydrogen with respect not to chlorine but to carbon: while each atom of one is satisfied with an atom of hydrogen, in the other each atom has capacity for four atoms of hydrogen. But it is *always the same* atomic *life,* the *same impotence to procure proximity for itself;* the hydrogen is the *same punctual reality* for both. The proximity intensifies only by means of the presence of future determinations, a presence that in the present each time procures the future proximity: this is the proximity of distant things (see Part One, Chapter II). The other is not intensification but multiplication.

*The naked eye sees the same as the telescope or microscope; the ear the same as the telephone or microphone.* Thus also all the instruments that register, with the precision of their intelligence, the signs of minimal relations drawn near by multiplied proximity—they grasp no more.

Isaiah would say about modern scientists: "*They have microscopes but do not see, they have microphones but do not hear.*"[77]

There is an experiment a scientist wanting objectivity can perform: he places himself in mortal danger and, instead of losing his head in infinite fear, has the courage not to fear until the very end: then *he will cut life at its thickest point,* affirm himself as finite in that infinity where others are torn apart by fear, and *know what life is.* Advisable, for example, is Gilliatt's experiment in *Les travailleurs de la mer,* when, sitting on the reef, he lets himself be killed by the rising water.[78] The living mortal tide bubbles around the man on the reef, lapping against him as it grows higher, ever more slowly, because it does not rise for a body but for the infinite will to *remain,* until at the last infinitesimal moment time *stops infinitely.* And then the man, who has raised his head by a thread to catch his breath and continue, will be able to deem himself in finite possession of the *infinita potestas:* he will *know* himself and will have absolute objective knowledge, in oblivion. Having performed the act of liberty, he will have *acted* with persuasion and not *suffered* his own need to live.

But this again would be catastrophic objectivity, and after all it is not necessary to design such a situation by artifice: that reef submerged by the tide is in the life of everyone, as is the air everyone reaches for in order to go on, ever forward, believing himself safe, because *nativity is the mortal accident,* and in life everyone can show to what degree he is blind and in the sway of things or to what degree he has reason in himself and sees his own destiny and that of others. Everyone can stop turning in the slavery of what he does not know and, refusing the pay-off of empty words, *have it out with life.*

## iii

But men fear this more than accidental death: *they fear life more than death.* They willingly renounce self-affirmation in determinate modes, provided that their renunciation has a name, a guise, a *persona* through which they may be given a vaster future—a crisis more distant and certain because of the force of others—and, at the same time, a nearer task, an activity that, feigning small goals attainable little by little in the near future, gives the illusion of walking to the man who stands still.

For the sake of a name, for the semblance of a *persona,* men willingly sacrifice their determinate demand, sensing un-certainty, and, intimidated, they abandon themselves to what-ever brutish exertion presents itself: *within each man hides the soul of a fakir.*

They need to see a stretch of road right before their eyes, presumably leading to some good, which certainly *defers* open *pain,* and, in continuing, flees from the abyss of cessation.

Therefore, each path forged is a new mine, each banner a mantle covering the insufficiency of the wretched, conceding to them a *persona* and a right: *thus does rhetoric flourish irresistibly.*

The closer and more easily completed the task, the more

diffuse the method and the more accepted and highly considered it is among men. The desert becomes a cloister, the banquet an academy, the artist's studio a school of beaux arts, because the toil of the rites takes on the name of sanctity; the wielding of concepts assumes the name of knowledge; imitative technique assumes the name of art; *any virtuosity assumes the name of a virtue.* (For it is simpler and profitable to train the fingers to a desperate acrobaticism than to understand what is played). *Virtuosity* is identical to *specialty:* I repeat, overstate, monstrously unfold a given act, a certain series of acts—and I have a noteworthy *persona.* I have trained an exceptional machine in myself. And the brutish, obscure toil *of the minimal life* has the same *name and right to exist* as the postulate *of the maximal life.*

In the degeneration of the knowing *persona,* through the re-search of knowledge, science, with its inexhaustible matter and its method made of the proximity of small, finite goals—with its cognitive self-positioning, which objectively tests and always repeats the same minimal reaction of the organism (which not only does not demand but does not tolerate the entire *persona*)—with its need of specialization, has taken root in the depth of man's weakness and *given the rhetoric of knowledge a solid constitution for all the coming centuries.* In the infinite sum of things that they do not see, men of science carry, with the tenacity of experimentation, the brief light of their dark lantern, in order to glean little by little from the simultaneity or succession of a given series of relations a presumption of causality: a modest hypothesis, which should become theory or law. *Law of what?* Law that in the given coincidence of given relations, the given thing happens at the given point. But how is it given and *what for?*—"*Because . . . ,*" they answer, struggling to derive a new law with new experiments. And at each "what for?" they answer "because," forging with difficulty, step by step, their paths of infinite causality, each in his burrow. It is the tale of Stento, repeating all the preceding steps to add one tiny step more.[79] It is true that thus did the Hebrews circle around Jericho without attacking it until the walls crumbled, but the Hebrews—then!—had a god who didn't fool around. Men of science have the god of philopsychia, pleasure, whose life consists of fooling everything that lives just in order to live.

But from the obscure extremity of their burrows each sends to the center the conquered "truths," for no matter how *one departs from the center, his life is itself a branching of the system,* and "truths" that arrive in this way are already defined and labeled such as to be part of the body of science. And to the first and fundamental "what for?" a sufficient response is feigned in the promise of infinite *becauses:* "the laws of matter such as they really exist and such as will be revealed to the indefatigable, objective research"; in the same manner, whenever the series of *becauses* is interrupted, a καλλώπισμα ὄρφνης, 'ornament of the darkness,' is imposed on the extremity, so that it stands as a pawn of the infinite *becauses* to be answered by science. But if "matter," the haze of correlativity, is an infinity οὗ οὐδὲν ἔξω, 'beyond which there is always something,' the way of science is an infinity οὗ ἀεί τι ἔξω, 'beyond the bounds of which lies nothing'; for at every point it must be finite in its affirmations. Because it will be finite in the infinite, it is infinite in each of its presumptions of finitude.

"But it does not presume to be finite; on the contrary, it professes its infinite way, and therefore each scientist in his given work is perfectly *honest.*" Thus the men of science indignantly protest, and with them a good share of laymen.

What's the use? The premise of the work is dishonest; the sufficiency of a finite work is dishonest at every point, even if it proceeds along a path professed as infinite in order to satisfy the demand of persuasion (it is dishonest for this very reason).

Whatever thing a scientist *indicates* as part of science, in the infinite correlativity of what lacks being, he will always say *unredliches,*[80] something that, in being inadequate to the demand, is dishonest to say.* And from the veil of his καλλω-πίσματα, 'ornaments,' which are "matter," "law," "finality," "vital principle," etc., he will always call out the same request in the same manner, a request he will have violated and blunted in his life because, in the activity of experiment, he feigns sufficient life.

True, science no longer makes dogmatic affirmations. The time is gone when, in order to keep growing, with violence† it had to break the arms of those who had learned how to embrace it with greater breadth. Its life is no longer a succession of exclusions and rebellions.

But this perpetual confession of insufficiency is nothing but the ultimate artifice for making itself more certain of its

---

*If I ask, "What is *bread?*" and answer, "Bread is what sates me," I have given an answer that is *right* for my hunger, for the continuation of my life. But this answer occurs *without words.* I experience hunger, take the bread, eat, and am quiet. But if I ask, I don't experience hunger for the bread but for something that can sate my hunger more lastingly than does a piece of bread. And to this hunger the answer that hints at satiety is *inadequate.*

What would be adequate for this hunger is the answer that tells me what good bread sates my hunger for, what good end my life continues for, so that bread too has an end sufficient to its existence. With my question I ask of the bread a taste other than the one that is sweet for my stomach. Now, if one feigns sufficient knowledge in affirming that bread sates me *because* it contains such and such substances, and it contains them because it's made of flour, and flour is obtained from such and such grains, and the grains . . . , he'll be able to say many things, but he'll be saying things that *do not want to be said,* he will say what is "*unredliches.*"

†I say *violence* because there is no other way for a new theory to triumph than by placing more and more people in contact with the particular quality of experiment that would demonstrate it.

future. Now it not only affirms a relation κατὰ, 'according to,' these circumstances of time and place but also adds κατὰ, this degree of our studies. It gets rid of its own *persona* in order for the method to remain intact, the right of *the work*, since that is the vital point, the reason, the absolute: the god, from which each derives the right to exist, the right, that is, to degrade oneself in a diminished life, in obtuse toil, to bend one's back in an obscure corner so as not to have to face life and not see death.

The rhetoric of science is the affirmation of this work, which is nothing but *referring to the deficiency* of things as if it were sufficient to the *demand of persuasion*. Yet in being the reason of the irrational, it repeats the irrational with modes and words that only on the true way of persuasion have a reason for being.[81]

## iv

In persecuting elementary relations through their accidental occurrence in order to note regularity, scientists relive the inorganic life of things not in what it shares with man—the impossibility of persuasion—but in relative persuasion, in determinations, in "properties," and in the modes in which they affirm themselves. Using quantities isolated from the rest, they can feign the regularity of a correlation disturbed in nature by other elements, *eliminating the contingency and procuring the proximity* so that the relation *occurs* regularly.

And because, moreover, they also abstract the elementary determinations of man, they can, in the interest of the latter, feign a full, complete reality, an ἐντελέχεια, 'entelechy,'[82] which culminates in the satisfaction of these needs and eliminates for scientists the usual contingencies. Thus, they give modern man medicine for his ills and the foresight that, without his power, draws near what he may need, a more secure satisfaction of his needs. This is clear in the machines that transform, bind, and eliminate the contingency from a certain circle of relations and, like an organic nucleus, afford proximity to the single part, so that the whole should conspire in the occurrence of the things man demands for himself. In this manner, like the latest of conscripts, scientists can *violate nature* better than others, to the greater comfort of the man wanting to go on.

And in social life, in the rapport between man and man, they abstract elementary necessities, are able to persecute them in their tiniest details and keep the statistics of good and bad in their *registries*. By attributing value to every determination, they point the way to the elimination of attrition, so that one *persona* may affirm himself not to the detriment but to the advantage of another. They do as the bees that carry pollen from flower to flower.

Above all, however, by means of the activity of scientists *certain words* infiltrate life as signs of given relations, given words on which men unknowingly prop themselves for their daily needs, and without knowing them they pass them on as they were received. *Technical terms* give men a certain uniformity of language. In vain do the proponents of intentionally created international languages dream. The international language *will be the language of technical terms;* of καλλωπίσματα ὄρφνης, 'ornaments of the darkness.'

Thus do laymen sing the praises of scientists as "pioneers of civilization." I say that they, in whom the voice of elementary needs speaks, procuring for itself the future proximity, are unconscious instruments in the development of the κοινωνία κακῶν, 'the community of the wicked,' by which men, though unable to understand one another, will certainly manage to come to an understanding.

# III
# Rhetoric in Life

TRANSLATORS' NOTE: *In the first portion of this chapter Michelstaedter satirizes the self-satisfaction of the "man of the world," who takes himself to be learned, tasteful, and attentive to duties; who relies on the perks of office, the prospect of a state pension, insurance, and medical science to cushion him against the human condition; and who is, from Michelstaedter's point of view, entirely fatuous. The satire of the thoroughly modern man takes the form of a Leopardian dialogue between such a person and an incredulous interlocutor, reaching its culminating* reductio ad absurdum *when the self-satisfied gentleman claims to have insured himself against death by merely taking out life insurance.*

*The attack is reminiscent of, and may well be modeled after, Søren Kierkegaard's critique of the modern bourgeois in* Concluding Unscientific Postscript: The Present Age. *Like Kierkegaard, Michelstaedter points to Hegel's characterization of the modern man in the* Philosophy of History *as a rich source. Like Kierkegaard, too, he seems to implicate Hegel's (and Croce's) notion that "the rational is the real and the real rational"* *as a justification for* *such fatuousness.*

*The question of the extent to which someone actually can fool* *himself in this way is on the table—as it also is in Tolstoy's later* *works, for example,* Resurrection, The Death of Ivan Ilych, *with* *which Michelstaedter was well acquainted. Michelstaedter's way of* *putting the question is to ask how deeply rhetoric can penetrate one's* *identity. His answer is that if humans are essentially social, as Hegel* *thinks, there is no limit at all: one must go to the other side of an as-* *ymptotic limit to find someone who is truly persuaded. That is what* *Michelstaedter means by "the other side of the hyberbola." Mo-* *dernity being, by definition, a network of mutual imbrication that* *uses economic means to cocoon everyone into illusory forms of secu-* *rity, the implication is that the present age cannot help but be "the* *reign of rhetoric."*

*Michelstaedter's argument depends, moreover, on an inter-* *pretation of Hegel's famous master-slave dialectic from the* Phe-nomenology of Mind, *as read through Marxist eyes. The previous* *chapter dealt with the conceptual structures necessary for under-* *standing modern science, as do the beginning chapters of Hegel's* Phenomenology. *Hegel thinks of the human world as emerging* *from the animal world by means of the master-slave dialectic. That* *is presumably why Michelstaedter, following his textual sources, ex-* *plains the universal dependence of people on one another in terms of* *masters and slaves. The master makes himself master by appropri-* *ating the labor power of the slave. The slave goes along with this be-* *cause he is unwilling to risk his physical life for his freedom. The* *slaves have truly inherited the world, as Marx predicted they would.* *But for Michelstaedter they nevertheless remain slaves because they* *are cosseted in the modern bonds of persuasion, which is to say, the*

*quest for material security in the company of the modern "herd."*
*Humans so love their physical life (philopsychia) that they are in no*
*way ready to risk any security that presents itself. They are thus com-*
*pared to mere animal life.*

*The "assimilatory organs" of the final segment are the social*
*parallel of the individual "stomachs preoccupied with the future"*
*discussed above. The former maintain the conspiracy of the weak*
*against the strong and generate modern society. They "take things*
*in" to transform them into food, as plants and animals do. Most*
*striking in this connection is Michaelstaedter's characterization of*
*the strong, who see their fellows as intrinsic rather than instrumen-*
*tal goods and whose activity, "turned toward life," may be under-*
*stood as a transformation of the Nietzschean will-to-power: Michel-*
*staedter envisions instead a "will-to-love."*

*Note that the texts on which Michelstaedter comments in con-*
*structing and critiquing the modern condition are modern ones.*
*Thus at the end of the work we see him move from meditating on*
*pre-Socratic sources to meditating on contemporary ones, in the*
*light of the deep wisdom he ascribes to the ancients but finds in con-*
*genial souls such as Leopardi.*

ἢ περὶ κακῶν κοινωνίας,

*or, on the community of the wicked*

φιλοψυχία κοινωνίαν συνέστησεν

*pleasure has generated society*

*of the many,*

*sad and wretched all, they make a people,*

*joyous and happy*

—Leopardi[83]


# i. The Individual in Society

## 1. THE OTHER SIDE OF THE HYPERBOLA

$$(x_{01}y_{01} = m^2)$$

"You see"—a portly gentleman said to me after an abundant dinner at the end of a long speech—"You see, life also has its good sides. One must know how to take it, not insist rigidly on what's already passed but adapt reasonably, and enjoy what our time offers, which no time before has ever offered to its children. One must take advantage of this marvelous comfort of living, and select from the increased variety of pleasures with wise moderation; *habere, non haberi,* 'to possess, not be possessed,' as they say."

"You are an artist, sir!"

"Yes, indeed, I believe I am; not that I write or draw. You understand: an artist . . . of the soul. I have a good heart, full of kind feelings. I make every situation poetic. I make life beautiful for myself, create my own pleasures. . . ."

"According to your fancy. . . ."

"Not as an eccentric, mind you! In the means and manner our generous life offers—easy and permissible."

"Reveling, but a man of the world."

"Certainly, but reveling . . . let's be clear! One must allow the body something and the spirit something. Poetry and literature have always been my passion. History too! There's real satisfaction in thinking, 'There, all of this, we made it,' and, on the other hand, in recognizing how far our life has come in evolving to the present degree of civilization. It's a fine thing, history. Who knows, if I hadn't got caught up in the administrative machinery. . . . Well. In any case, I do believe the way things are going today, every man who wants to keep up with progress has to possess a varied and select humanistic culture. Nor should one be entirely ignorant of the exact sciences, in which we're the true masters of creation. No mystery escapes us any longer!"

"But you're so many-sided!"

"Oh, an amateur . . ."

"You find time for everything!"

"Certainly. But one must be conscious of doing one's duty. That much is certain. On duty one doesn't compromise. It's one thing to get satisfaction from literature, science, art, and philosophy in pleasant conversations—but serious life is something else. You could say: theory is one thing, practice another! For myself, as you see, I get satisfaction from these theoretical discussions and take real pleasure in elegant ethical problems, and even allow myself the luxury of exchanging some paradoxical propositions. But don't mistake—everything in its time and place. When I wear the uniform, I wear another *persona*. I believe that in the exercise of his functions man must be absolutely free. Free in mind and spirit. In the antechamber of my office I leave all my personal opinions, feelings, human weaknesses. And I enter the temple of civilization to accomplish my work with a heart tempered by objectivity! Then I feel I'm bringing my contribution to the great work of civilization for the good of humanity. And the holy institutions speak through me. Am I right, eh?"

"I admire your firmness. But . . . you don't think of your own interests?"

"Wages flow and are certain. And then, you know, the perks . . ."

"Right, yes, but . . . then when—god forbid—this admirable fiber of yours weakens?"

"There's a pension: the State doesn't abandon its faithful, eh?"

"But—sorry if I put unpleasant images in your head—but we're weak men. In case of sickness, you know, there are so many around nowadays . . ."

"Not at all. I belong to a welfare fund, like all my colleagues. Our hospital has all the modern conveniences, and one gets treated according to the most modern attainments of medicine. See?"

"Oh, I see! But, I don't know, so many things can happen. I understand that we're protected by laws, but still, thefts are common."

"I am insured against theft."

"Ah, well, and . . . suppose there's a fire."

"Insured against fire."

"Goodness! But horse—sorry, I mean, *automobile*—accidents, or roof tiles . . ."

"Insured against accidents."

"But then death. We all die!"

"Not at all. I'm insured in case of death."

Then he added triumphantly, smiling at my bewilderment, "As you see, I'm secure in a locked vault, as they say."

I was speechless. But in my bewilderment the idea flashed through my mind that before it is placed in a vault, wine must pass through a press.

This man of his time[*]—with his προθυμία, 'busy-ness' and his "locked vault"—is the individual dreamed of by Hegel who stands at the top of the Gothic church of which the ancients were ignorant,[†] at the final moment of the free evolution of the system of liberty;[‡] he is the objectification of the liberty that is its own end and its own enjoyment;[¶] and "the *persona* he dons" in the exercise of his office, that is, his second nature,[§] his moral freedom, the concrete means by which the idea and

[*]Hegel, *Philosophie der Geschichte,* Rekl. Bibl., 4881–85 (I do not translate the citations from Hegel because I have no hope of reproducing in Italian their ineffable kallopismatism): "Die Lebendigkeit des Staates in den Individuen ist Sittlichkeit genannt worden. Der Staat, seine Gesetze, seine Einrichtungen sind der Staatsindividuen Rechte; . . . Alles ist iher Besitz ebenso, wie sie von ihm besessen werden, denn es macht ihre Substanz, iher Sein aus" (p. 93). 'The life of the state in individuals is called morality. The state, its laws, its institutions are the rights of the individuals of the state. [ . . . ] Everything is their property, just as they in turn are also possessed by it, for it constitutes their substance, their being.'

[†]"Von solchem gotischen Dombau haben die Alten nichts gewusst" (p. 88). [The phrase is translated by Michelstaedter in the text. All page numbers refer to Reklam's *Universalbibliotek* edition of Hegel's work, employed by Michelstaedter.—Translators' note.]

[‡]"Das System der Freiheit (ist) freie Entwicklung ihrer Momente" (p. 88). 'The system of liberty is the free development of its moments.'

[¶]"Die Freiheit is sich der Zweck, den sie ausführt" (p. 54). 'Liberty is the end it pursues.' "Er (der Staat) ist so der Weltgeschichte überhaupt, worin die Freiheit ihre Obiectivität erhält und im Genusse dieser Obiectivität lebt" (p. 78). 'The state is therefore the object most immediately determined with respect to universal history, where liberty acquires its objectification and lives in the enjoyment of its objectification.'

[§]"Die Sittlichkeit aber ist die Pficht, das substantielle Recht, *die zweite Natur,* wie man sie mit Recht genannt hat, denn die erste Natur des Menschen ist sein unmitelbares, tierisches Sein" (p. 78). 'But morality is duty, substantial right, *second nature,* as it is rightly called, for the first nature of man is his immediate, animal existence.'

the human passions are united,* the essential end of subjective existence, the union of subjective will and *rational will,* this is the divine idea,† that which God meant to do with the world in order to regain himself.‡ Yet I believe that hunger, sleep, and fear—even if they are called "rational will"—remain always hunger, sleep, and fear, and so do all other things because of which I do not know where the bounds of our egoism might be untroubled,⁙ egoism that to the extent it is such cannot be bounded;[84] nor do I know where "moral liberty" or "the idea" or "the essential end" might be.

    *"Die konkrete Mitte und Vereinigung beider (der Idee und der menschlichen Leidenschaften) ist die sittliche Freiheit im Staate" (p. 59). 'Moral liberty in the state forms the concrete center and junction of the two elements: the idea and the human passions.'
    †"*Der Staat ist die göttliche Idee, wie sie auf Erden vorhanden ist*" (p. 78). '*The state is the divine idea as it exists on earth.*'
    ‡"Dieser Endzweck ist das, was Gott mit der Welt will, Gott aber ist das Volkommenste und kann darum nichts als sich selbst, seinen eignen Willen wollen" (p. 54). 'This ultimate end is what God wants with the world, but God is what is most perfect and can want nothing but himself, his own will.' But: "Quidve novi potuit tanto post ante quietos / inlicere ut cuperent vitam mutare priorem? / Nam gaudere novis rebus debere videtur / cui veteres obsunt: sed cui nil accidit aegri / tempore in anteacto, cum pulchre degeret aevom, / quid potuit novitatis amorem accendere tali?" (Lucretius, v, 168). 'And what novel incident should have induced them hitherto to rest so long after to desire to change their former life? For it seems natural he should rejoice in a new state of things, whom old things annoy; but for him whom no ill has befallen in times gone by, when he passed a pleasant existence, what could have kindled in such a one a love of change?' [Lucretius 63—Translators' note.]
    ⁙From the disheartening contemplation of the blood-soaked paths of history, we comfort ourselves thus: "dass wir in die Gegenwart unsrer Zwecke und Interessen, kurz in die Selbstsucht zurücktreten, welche am ruhigen Ufer steht und von da aus sicher des fernen Anblicks der verworrenen Trümmermasse geniesst" (p. 56). 'In the actuality of our ends and interests, in egoism, which rejoices in the security of the calm bank at the distant spectacle of the confused mass of ruins.'

"But," says my man, "what do I care about all that? I know I'm secure, free, and strong in the consciousness of my rights and duties." Or, in the words of John Stuart Mill (*On Liberty*), "The subject [here] is not the so-called Liberty of the Will, so unfortunately opposed to the misnamed doctrine of *Philosophical Necessity;* but Civil or Social Liberty."* The "liberty of being a slave," then? Fine.

Indeed, it is this that man searches for; this is how he believes he will attain joy, and he cannot exit from himself in order to see more than this. But he pays for his ignorance with a slow, obscure, and continuous torment, which he does not confess and which others do not see, for destiny is like an equation and does not lend itself to deception.

It is the other side of the hyperbola.† Man is still alive,

*These are the first words of the first chapter (Rekl. Bibl., 3491–92). [Mill's sentence concludes with a further specification of his topic: "the nature and limits of the power which can be legitimately exercised by society over the individual."—Translators' note.]

†At limit $C_1$ = pleasure without life. $x$ = the pretense of certain pleasure (sufficiency, presumption of right). $y$ = individual action. $x_{01}$ = lim $x$ = ∞: finite security of one's own pleasures through infinite contingencies.

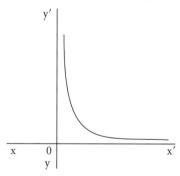

$y_{01}$ = lim $y$ = 0: elimination of activity (personal obligation). $xy = m^2$: life is an irreducible greatness, and society draws infinitely near to this limit but never reaches it.

still occupies space, and must still perform some little thing in order to sense the postulate of security as infinite.

Whereas with the first side man never felt able to justly demand something as just to himself, here he always presumes the sufficiency of whatever *persona* he has; and whereas the other postulated justice in liberation from the irrational will, this man seeks security in his adaptation to a code of rights and duties: the liberty of being a slave. Whereas the first demanded *present* satisfaction all at once, this searches for the means of continuing securely to have hunger in all the future. And whereas the first way was that of the greatest individuals, demanding value and resembling it in their free and indestructible will, the latter is the way of the individual's disintegration and of those who worry about life as if it had value (sufficiency), living ὡς ἐόντος, 'as if there were' the absolute, with foresight limited to the moment. For one loves and turns his gaze toward total possession, identity, and the other is touched and overconscientious about what he thinks he possesses—in order that it should remain for him in the future. But to the extent that he possesses it, that much is he possessed by it. "*And he turns back toward the things that are behind him.*" Remember the wife of Lot, says Christ. Ὃς ἂν ζητήσῃ τὴν ψυχὴν αὐτοῦ περποιήσασθαι, ἀπολέσει αὐτήν* (St. Luke).[85] This is the path each man opens if he wants to procure for himself the pleasure of life (see Part One, Chapter II). But here we find individuals reduced to mechanisms, foresight actuated in the organism, not however, as we might expect, as victims of their weakness, in the grip of chance, but as "sufficient" and as certain as divinity. Their degeneration is called civil education,

---

*This is untranslatable because of the effect of περί, *medio*, 'mean,' and the double sense of ψυχή, 'spirit-soul,' 'life' (whosoever seeks to *ensure for himself the conservation* of his own *persona* will bring it to dissolution).

their hunger is the activity of progress, their fear is morality, their violence and egoistic hatred—the sword of justice: ὀρφνης καλλωπίσμασιν ἀνθεῖ κακῶν περ ὕπουλος ἡ πρὸς βίον κοινωνία, 'with the ornaments of the darkness, society, internally corrupt and reaching for life, will blossom'; and διὰ τὸ τὴν τέχνην καλῶς ἐξεργάζεσθαι ἕκαστος ἠξίου καὶ τἆλλα τὰ μέγιστα σοφώτατος εἶναι, 'on the strength of their poetry they believed themselves to be the wisest of men in other things in which they were not wise.'*

For them Christ said, εἰ τυφλοὶ ἦτε, οὐκ ἂν εἴχετε ἁμαρτίαν· νῦν δὲ λέγετε ὅτι βλέπομεν· ἡ ἁμαρτία ὑμῶν μένει, 'if you were blind, you would not be guilty, but because you say, "We see," your guilt remains.'†

They have made themselves a force from their weakness, for by speculating on this common weakness they have created a security out of reciprocal convention.

It is the reign of rhetoric.

Indeed, to the degree that each man is limited to the moment, society extends its foresight in space and time so that each might be able κοινωφελῶς φιλοψυχεῖν, 'to be attached to life' in a socially useful manner, to think—each in his own little place—about his own little life. But this is only possible in such a determinate manner that every other in turn might do as much, rotating on his own pivot and tasting a little at a time through his teeth the teeth of the interconnected wheels, ὁρμῶντές τε καὶ ὁρμώμενοι, 'moved and moving at one and the same time,' infallible and certain all, inasmuch as through their life lives the great organism, with its complex and exquisite foresight, crystallized in the delicate and powerful minds who eliminate from the field of life every contingency.

*Plato, *Apology* 22d.
†John 9:41.

When one puts a coin into a mechanical organ and turns the correct lever, the machine plays the desired melody (because the composer's musical genius and the technical genius of the organist are crystallized in its gears); likewise, in exchange for the determinate labor a man performs for society, which is familiar and instinctive to him in manner but obscure in reason and in end, society lavishes on him *sine cura* all that is necessary to him. For in the social organization all the genius of the strongest individuals accumulated over the centuries is crystallized: ὁ βίος ὁ μετ' ἀσφαλείας ἥδιστος, 'life with security is the sweetest.'*

## 2. SECURITY

$$(\lim c_1 \, x = \infty)$$

The security of necessary things consists of the power to ensure the future affirmation of one's own determinations in the face of all other external and hostile determinations (forces): to defeat matter (time and the diversity of things in space) with one's own form.

In such matter my fellow creatures are also included: they are distinguished from the rest of matter in determining themselves the same way that I do; that is, in order *to continue* they impose on the rest of matter the same form I impose on it.

Thus, *security* (the 'res,' or "thing," as men of the law put it) means

    1. violence against nature: labor.
    2. violence toward man: property.

*Aristotle,' Ρητορικά, Α 5, 15. [Aristotle, *Rhetoric* I.5.1360b15.—Translators' note.]

1. I work the field or take advantage of the sun, rain, air, and earth, kill harmful animals, and domesticate those that may be of use to me. I pick the fruit of the earth, violating the plant; I construct a roof for protection against the elements and the wild beasts, overcoming space and inertia and the hardness of the stone; I make clothes, arms, tools; I hunt game in the forest, cut wood for cooking at my hearth, eating it along with the fruits of my field to my greater glory.

As long as there are air, earth, sun, and water, and fields and forests on the earth with animals and vegetation, the potentiality of work in me and the accumulation of past labor (elaborated things) in my possession are sufficient security for my future. But here is the greatest danger before which I have no foresight; here is a potentiality of work identical to mine that wants to be fixed at the same point in space and time and that takes all my future from me: here is man, my *fellow creature.*

2. The battle is resumed, the field still smoke-filled. The two men contend for the security of being able to violate nature and make use of the accumulation of past labor. In short, the fellow creatures are no longer fellow, but one has the right of labor or *proprietà immobile,* 'real estate,' and the right to accumulate labor or *proprietà mobile,* 'movable property'; one has affirmed his individuality before the other, and the other has his *future cropped* and is at the *mercy* of the victor in that he wants to live and cannot take advantage of his own labor power. The other then gives him the means of living, provided that he works for him. Thus has man subordinated his fellow creature to his own security: he has extended his violence to his fellow so that the latter should cooperate in providing him with what he needs. And this latter, the slave, is matter before the master—he is a *thing.*

But he is a "thing" in a manner different from the way a

tree is a "thing" that the master uproots in order to use for its wood. He is a "thing" like a tree that the master grafts and prunes in order to harvest its fruit, like one that he periodically deprives of branches in order to have firewood. The slave is useful to the master alive even in order to die for him—but not dead.

Thus, his slavery is not absolute but relative to his need to live. The hand of the slave is not forced to turn the mill grindstone, but it does so in order that the body should have food to eat and not, by whip or torture, be prevented from doing it temporarily or for good. Inherent in each of the coercive means or in the threat of coercive means is the victorious violence of the master, absolute persuasiveness with regard to the slave's will to live.

The slave who no longer needs the future is free because he no longer gives a foothold to the persuasion of the master's violence. As long as water has weight, the will to go to the earth's center, it can be constrained to make mills run, and factories will be huddled on banks: it must follow all the ways prepared by man and make all his wheels turn if it wants to descend and not remain suspended. But the day the water no longer needs "what is below," man's sluices, canals, and wheels will be in vain, and all his factories and mills will remain forever still.

The master makes use *of the slave through his form, through his labor power.* He makes him feel that his *right* to exist coincides with the sum of duties toward the master; his *security* is conditioned by his uninterrupted adherence to the needs of the master.

In his hard but secure chains, therefore, the slave acquires security among men through the violation of nature to the master's advantage, and through his violence against his fellow creature the master derives security before nature from him, which he, because he does not work, no longer has in himself. United, they are both secure; detached, they both die: because one has the right but not the power of labor; the other, the power but not the right.

But the code says: "Each man has by nature rights self-evident to reason";* it declares that everything may be considered a *thing* but that man is not a *thing* (§285) but a *persona*, and it proclaims the *liberation of slaves* (§16).

Men *will have* to love one another? Each sacrifice his own future for his companion? Or must the bloody battle explode again, each being obliged to conquer his own future at the risk of losing it?

The insecure masters and insecure freedmen look at one another in terror, the former nostalgic for a secure dominion, the latter for secure chains.

Love and open strife threaten their security in one and the same manner. But society opens its maternal arms and is in fact concerned only for this security. Its code speaks this way "for convenience"; in reality it is only the crystallization of the individual's preoccupation with his future. The Eskimo and the Ethiopian meet in the temperate zone and cry out simultaneously. "I'm cold," says the Ethiopian, "give me your skins"; "I'm hot," says the Eskimo, "give me your feathers." Each sees in the other only the *thing* necessary to him, not the man who

---

*I cite the 1905 edition of the Austrian Code, §16. "Jeder Mensch hat angeborne schone durch die Vernunft einleuchtende Rechte und ist daher als eine *Person* zu betrachten. Sklaverei oder Leibeigenschaft und die Ausübung einer darauf sich beziehenden Macht wird in diesen Ländern nicht gestattet." 'Each man has by nature rights evident to reason in and of themselves and consequently should be considered a *person*. Servitude or slavery of people is not authorized in our lands, nor is the exercise of power that might be linked to such.'

must himself live (for in that case each ought to suppose that the thing necessary to him is necessary to the other as well). But the preoccupation with his own life keeps each from compromising his entire self in the struggle. The exchange suitable to both makes them secure, albeit without mutual love, without anyone's victory. And society takes care that an Eskimo always meets an Ethiopian in this way, thereby guaranteeing that each of its feeble children, without fighting, has his soup, which he would not know how *to make for himself* or, once it were made, *defend it from others.*

I am weak in body and soul. Placed in the midst of nature I would quickly fall victim to hunger, the elements, wild beasts. Placed in possession of what I need, sheltered from the forces of nature but in the midst of other men's greed, I would be quickly deprived of everything and perish miserably. Society takes me, teaches me how to move my hands according to established rules and, for this miserable labor of my miserable machine, flatters me, saying I am a person, I have acquired rights solely on account of my being born, gives me all that I need and not mere sustenance but all the refined products of others' labor: it gives me security in the face of all others. Men have found in society a better master than individual masters because it does not demand of them a variety of labor, a potency sufficient to the security before nature, but only a small, simple bit of labor, familiar and obscure, provided one performs it in the necessary manner, provided one does not clash with the interests of the master: εἰ ἐλευθέρους αὐτοὺς δει / ζῆν, τῶν κρατούντων ἐστὶ πάντ᾽ ἀκουστέα, 'If they are to live in freedom, they must obey in all things those who hold power.'[86] Security is easy but that much harder; society has well-determined methods: it binds, limits, threatens. Its diffuse strength is concrete in that masterpiece of persuasion— the penal code. The concern for security enslaves man in every act. From the moment he wants to say, "This is legally mine," he has by means of *his own future* made himself a slave *to the future of all the others: he is matter* (personal property).

But in exchange, society does what no master would: it makes its slaves participants in its own authority by transforming their labor into money and giving money the force of law. "Jedermann ist unter den von den Gesetzen vorgeschriebenen Bedingungen fähig Rechte zu erwerben," 'Whosoever finds himself within the prescribed conditions of the law is capable of exercising rights' (§18). The possibility of acquiring a right to a thing already elaborated so that it is useful to man, to an accumulation of the labor of others, is already a de facto right to the labor of others. The possibility of acquiring the right to *bearbeiten,* 'belabor,' a thing (real estate), insofar as it means that others will not work, is the de facto right to someone else's *nonlabor.* Property is therefore violence against the person of another and, through that person, against nature. This violence is absolute among men. For society vindicates, with all its might, the rights of its faithful.

"Jedem der sich in seinem Rechte gekränkt zu sein erachtet steht es frei seine Beschwerde vor der durch die Gesetze bestimmten Behörde anzubringen," 'Whosoever considers himself injured in his proper right may claim restitution by the authorities designated by the law' (§19).

In this way, each individual can personally render absolute for himself the security he enjoys by general coercion. The meager will wants to affirm its determination. And society gives it the means of taking. The meager will cannot defend what it has taken by its own violence and entrusts its defense to the violence of society.

The meager will, ignoring all that is not the obscure sense of its necessities, (and which, because of these, ignores and denies any other will that τὸ ἑαυτῆς μέρος, 'for its part,' would kill everything living in order to continue living itself), acquires in this way, through society, intelligent and secure power over every other will, over everything that past centuries have made and the current century produces. Every other will is slave to its future. Everything is matter for its life.

In this manner, everyone in organized society violates everyone else by means of the omnipotence of the organization. Everyone is matter and form, slave and master at one and the same time, in that the common advantage imposes common duties and affords equal rights to all. The organization is omnipotent and incorruptible because it consists of the individual's deficiency and fear. And there is no greater power than that which turns its own weakness into strength. The individual who lives his life in the social mode for his own security, κοινωφελῶς φιλοψυχῶν, 'attached to life,' in a socially useful manner, who has found that the freedom of being a slave to life is secure for the man who knows how τοῖς κρατοῦσιν εἰκαθεῖν, 'to assimilate himself to those who hold power,' and who has adapted to the social form, is jealous of that form precisely because of the *weakness* through which he placed his trust in it; he is jealous in the same way that the creditor is jealous of his promissory note, who, in accepting it and entrusting his belongings to it, depends for his life on that piece of paper. For each is attached—the latter to the paper, the former to the social form—like a shipwreck victim to a saving plank, *not out of love for the plank but for his own salvation.* Thus do men, who have accepted society's promissory note, hold it with their benumbed fingers—or with the firmness of their principles—and hence derives their angry glance toward the opinion of others, the στάσις, 'firmness,' of every faith that might ἐπεγείρῃ στασιν τινά, 'stir up rebellion,' toward every deed that might become seditious; hence their solemnity, like

an orchestral instrument feeling the composer's authority because it blows and is blown—for which I am amazed they do
not all use "we" in place of "I" like traveling salesmen or bank
messengers who speak of "our millions"; hence their
ἀκρίβεια, 'exactitude,' in measuring rights and duties, their
"sufficiency," which cannot bear the fact that what is enough
for them is not for others, and if someone uses more than what
is given to all by common measure, they feel personally outraged.* This is why, if they had to sacrifice to a god other than
the eternal Pluto, they would sacrifice to Procustes.[87] One must
simply ask what those rights are which, according to the code,
are due to man according to rational evidence because he was
born, and what is a "*persona*."

## 3. THE REDUCTION OF THE PERSON

$$(\lim c_1 = y = 0)$$

Strolling along an old street of my city, I have often been en-
ticed by the pleasant view afforded by the façades. Even the
traces of time and inclement weather have a respectable and
comforting look. But cities, as is known, progress. New needs
culminate in building projects, and building projects merci-

---

*It is for this reason that "outrage" has taken on the meaning in com-
mon usage of *offense*. Not so the Greek ὕβρις, which remains confined to the
subject (as potency) and has in it its Nemesis (see *Hymn to Nemesis* by Meso-
mede); it assumes the viewpoint of the outraged; "offense," only in affirmations at a certain point with respect to a certain thing. (In the New Testa-
ment, by means of the immanence of the universal correlative "God" at every
point, ὕβρις means "offense" even without relation.) Thus the transitive of
the verb (which is precisely the affirmation at a certain point with respect to
a certain thing) ὑβρίζω τινα, 'I give offense to another.' Hence the substantives ὕβρισμα, ὑβρισμός, 'offense.'

lessly tear apart what stands in the way. My street has been respected, but all the buildings amassed behind the first line of houses on one side have been leveled, and along this side, to whoever now passes through the cleared area, the homes with respectable façades afford, alas, the whole desolate spectacle of their intimate squalor. Whoever has contemplated it once intuitively knows it when he passes again, even through the respectable façade.

Likewise, through the respectable façade that men on the path of mutual security present, we can intuit the squalor of reduced individuality. Thus do we proceed in our discussion of the formula to a consideration of the second variable.

*Der Unbeugsame wuchs nicht leichtsinnig auf,* as they say: "He who does not bend does not easily* grow."

Cedars that, under favorable conditions, grow taller and more quickly than their fiber can bear, once burdened with their own weight, soon bend their tops to the ground. But those that do battle with a thankless terrain and a hostile climate, if they have grown at all, have done so as much as their strength has permitted, and there is no wind that can bend them.

The man who has assumed the social *persona,* with which he has grown by usurping the inadequate security offered him by the atmosphere, has based his life on the contingency of things and people, and in living on the charity of these, he depends on them for his future and does not have in himself the strength to retain what—not because of his own value—belongs to him.

The more an individual adapts to circumstantial contingencies, that much less is it *his* sufficiency, because that much more restricted in him is the foresight diffused *per artus,*

---

* Ἐν εὐμαρείᾳ, 'amid comforts.'

'through his limbs.' To the degree that social foresight is broadened and sufficient to a greater number of contingencies, that much narrower is the sphere of foresight and limited the sufficiency of the individual who, for his own security, has entrusted himself to social foresight. Within the social individual, absolute social security corresponds to a foresight that is reduced to the instant and point such that, at every new insufficient contingency, the individual would perish wretchedly if he were removed from the bosom of society. All progresses of civilization are regresses for the individual.

Every technological progress dulls the body of man. Clothing, houses, and the artificial production of heat render useless the organism's faculty of reacting* to the air, heat, cold, the sun,† water.

Because of the ease of having food without procuring it for himself and the ease of weapons, the lone individual is no longer a dangerous force amid the animals. He no longer has either the agility or the articulated and measured strength or the thousands of shrewd maneuvers that reside in the potentiality of his body and made of man one of the most beautiful beasts of prey.

But society eliminates every πόνος, 'strain,' every danger whose defeat requires one's entire intelligent and tenacious

---

*The significance of the "Kneipp treatment"! [Sebastian Kneipp (1821–97) reportedly cured himself of tuberculosis by means of a self-designed holistic therapy, which consisted of cold-water immersion, exercise, and dietary control.—Translators' note.]

†To neutralize the damaging effects of the sun, exposed skin becomes tan; sheltered, it again becomes light. The skin of the face and hands, always exposed to variations, colors and loses color quickly. When the skin of the body is exceptionally exposed, it takes longer to color and retains color even when it has been sheltered. This delaying of reaction generally produces dangerous sunburns.

strain, the engagement of the entire self for survival, substitut-
ing instead either security or ἀμηχάνους συμφοράς, 'irreparable misfortunes'; because of this men do not triumph or succumb in battle but find themselves either safe or dead.
Society burdens itself with carrying the precious *persone*
of its children such that they should not strain. Thus, from the
man who, upright on the horse he has broken, controlling it by
the peculiar language of muscular quivers in his legs, and who
travels across unknown landscapes aware of the dangers and
prepared to react appropriately, or who passes through mountains, scaling vertiginously sloped walls, finding in every harsh-
ness a support sufficient to his hands and his feet articulated
like hands, skirting the abyss without allowing his heart to vac-
illate* and passing by landslides "without his foot displacing a
stone,"† to the bored traveler cooped up in a train car that,
bouncing him about, carries him above, below, through rivers
and mountains and plains, while he stretches and yawns or
talks about schedules with profound causal knowledge or dis-
putes with the conductor with the subtlest of arguments about
combined tickets, the supplement rate, the rights and mutual
obligations of travelers and railroad employees, while if divine
providence were to send him crashing into another train full
of passengers, half asleep but flying to meet him at sixty kilo-
meters per hour, he would not have time to swear before finding himself dead, passed directly from his petty connection

*I say "heart" as the French do because it has a decent ring to it, but
what I mean is "stomach."
†Baumbach, *Zlatorog: The Legend of Triglav.* [Rudolf Baumbach's
(1840–1905) *Zlatorog: Eine Alpensage* (1877) was based on the South Slav romantic tale of a chamois with golden horns and the "White Ladies," or
fairies, who kept the mountain pastures green and helped humans in
need.—Translators' note.]

times to the eternity of death, reduced, to his great indignation—him, civil man—to the level of his ancestral troglodytes
and all the other animals of creation; from the seaman with his
sail and rudder in hand, he being the reason for equilibrium
between wind and sea, who feels on his face the direction and
force of the wind and measures tack with his sure eye, who
struggles with the storm to overcome or die, to the passenger
on a transatlantic cruise ship, who, either as merchandise piled
up in the hold or as *high life* above deck, doubles up from sea-
sickness and, trusting in the overbearing strength of the ton-
nage and the boilers of the steamer, which stands like an island
in the storm, finds himself going down like a rock together
with all his companions without any possible struggle if a cliff
or the bow of another ship might take it upon itself to open the
sides of this floating city—between the former and the latter,
I mean to say, the difference is as great as that between organic
and mineral life.

Every substitution of machines for manual work dulls by
that amount the hands of man, for they were trained to know
how to do things from thought directed toward determinate
necessities; and by means of the contrivance in which that
thought was crystallized once and for all, they are rendered
useless and lose the intelligence of those necessities. Thus, for
instance, have blacksmiths become dulled in our days. At one
time they knew how to forge from a block of iron whatever
object you might have wished using fire, hammer, and chisel,
whereas today they barely know how to adapt and screw together the ready-made pieces from the factories or foundries
and no longer make even keys or nails themselves, so that one
finds hardly anyone who knows how to shoe a horse anymore;*

*It is true that this too is becoming a useless art.

and the master stonecutters, and carpenters, and weavers, etc. Their places have been taken by the masses of sad, dull factory laborers who know but one gesture, who are, it seems, the final lever of their machines.

In this manner, the photographer has replaced the engraver and will replace the painter, and the *phonole* and *orchestrion* will replace musicians.*

The eyes will end by not seeing what they would see in vain, the ears by not hearing what they would hear in vain: the body will disintegrate, emptying itself.[†]

So also in the activity of their whole self, the power of which is further concealed because it is not concrete and actively visible in the parts of the body, the sphere of individual activity has limited its influence to the extent that society's ra-

---

*Do not talk to me about the *sports* that are supposed to counterbalance all this. The reason for *sport*, its goal, is never in the doing but in the "having done": the religion of the *sportsman* is the "record." And "record" means (1) *the most partial development*, because one who wants to hold a record should not be thinking of anything else, (2) *danger without sufficiency* in all the *sports* in which man entrusts himself to a machine and makes it work to excess. Even the hunter is reduced to the man who has himself taken to a place where animals are driven before his nose so he can slaughter them . . . unless he wants to shoot at the legs of cattle drivers because this too ἔχει τέλος τι εὔχρηστον, 'has a useful end.' *Sports* reenter in this way the order of all other social things: dull and uniform labor; ἀμήχανος συμφορά, 'irreparable misfortunes,' substituted for πόνος, 'strain.' *Sports* are the rhetoric of physical life.

†An inkling of this process—at the very least, clearly an invention of society—may be found in the diseases of the limbs, the muscular diseases that arise generally from inertia and atrophy, and the diseases of the internal organs that result from their working alone without the measure that the vitality of the limbs used to give their activity, or from hypertrophy; connected to the latter are circulatory disorders: in general the disturbance of the organism's affirmation of existence, the assimilation of matter to its own form: *metabolic disorders*. The signs that life is out of focus are nervous disorders, of which society seems almost to boast.

dius has grown larger. Because here, too, the law that by de-
grees eliminates τὸν πόνον, 'strain,' dominates and provides
security interrupted only by ἀμήχανοι συμφοραί, 'irreparable
misfortunes,' men find themselves being either saved or fallen.
The words "Do not commit yourself entirely," "Distin-
guish between theory and practice," "Assume a *persona* with
the sufficiency given to you," "Measure duties and rights," "Conform to what is suitable," constitute the *pentalogue* of the social
man. This man, who has accepted society's promissory note
and packed it with the care of his own security, no longer has
the need of burdening himself with it; nor must he do so. The
code says that he who takes justice into his own hands will be
punished. But social man must no longer think about justice
at all. It does not concern him: *he is under protection—he has
no voice.* He must instead keep to the path that they have prepared for him. Where it leads is not his concern. He wears eye
guards like coach horses so as not to look to the right or left.
His foresight must be limited to the next little bit of road in
order not to stumble. In this manner, the *sense of responsibility*
is taken from him. A horse that carries a man to commit a
crime is not responsible for the crime; nor is our man responsible for the evil or the good that his going serves. He is not a
*Mitwisser,* συνειδώς, *conscius,* 'aware agent,' but an accessory
in good faith.

He cannot long remember the places through which he
has passed, absorbed as he is by the present accidents of the
way and by watching where to put his feet. Those regarded him
then, when he was passing; now he would be naive to think
about them and would lose the trail: *this is reality—practice;*
this is what his life depends on. There was someone walking
next to him who helped him at difficult passes. Another turned
up, knocking down the first and taking his place. Our walking

man cannot burden himself with the fallen one: he must think about where to put his feet. "Too bad," he says, continuing on as he tries to obtain the good will of the new companion and receive his help, just as he did in the case of the other. For he saw help in him, not a companion. Νήπιος ὅς τῶν οἰκτρῶς / οἰχομένων γονέων ἐπιλάθεται, says Electra: 'Foolish is the child who forgets a parent's piteous death' (ll. 145–46). Not a man but an infant, *unmündig,* is he who does not assume the ἀντίρροπον ἄχθος, the 'correlative weight,' of the pain that touched him through those who were linked to him. He is not responsible for what he once called his own. Because his *persona* of today is not that of yesterday, who can *give it responsible voice?* "But," says the walking man, "μηδὲν ἐπ᾽ ἀμήχανον, 'only as much as is possible'; I can't, I must not engage myself completely; these are nice little things; εἰ δ᾽ ἐλεύθερόν με δεῖ / ζῆν, τῶν κρατούντων ἐστὶ πάντ᾽ ἀκουστέα, 'If I am to live in freedom, I must obey in all things those who have power';[88] I must think about serious things." And on he goes, intent on the rocks of the way, which are seriousness, reality. But *that reality, the one of before, what is it to him?* The horse knows the reality of the rocks only with regard to its feet (see Part One, Chapter II; Part Two, Chapter II).

Thus are *the places through which* the walking man passes *commonplaces* to him. What does he know about the things he brushes in passing, the things on which he supports himself in order to go forward? What does he know about how they live or what they want or what they are? This alone he knows— whether they are hard or soft for him, difficult or easy, favorable or hostile. He ignores what is just to others, making use of things and people only ὃ κατὰ τὴν κοινωνίαν τυγχάνει νεμόμενος, that is, 'insofar as they are useful to his going.'

Yielding, waiting, settling and—in order not to engage himself and compromise all his future in a single point— forgetful and irresponsible, social man draws life (pulls himself ever forward), ignoring it until Jove should set him free.

Ὠκύμοροι, καπνοῖο δίκην ἀρθέντες ἀπέπταν,
αὐτὸ μόνον πεισθέντες, ὅτῳ προσέκυρσεν
    ἕκαστος,
πάντοσ᾽ ἐλαυνόμενοι.

Destined to a near death, they agitate and dissipate themselves like smoke / each believes only in what
    he has been
tossed onto / pressed on all sides.

Empedocles[89]

Somewhere it is written (in Schopenhauer, I believe) that he who could see to the heart of a pot of earth would see nothing but a dark tendency toward the bottom and an obscure cohesive force. And if he could see into the mind of a man he would see the entire world and all other men and himself. It is like saying that in the eye of a man facing a panorama the whole scene lives again in all its detail, but just as in the retina what lives clearly is only the point that ἄν, 'each time eventually,' is in focus, all the rest being uncertain because the eye sees it without seeing it but *certum habet*, 'has certitude,' only about what it has seen, so, I believe, the man who glanced into the mind of the average man would find there a truly strange and deformed image of the world and of men and himself: στεινωποὶ μὲν γὰρ παλάμαι κατὰ γυῖα κέχυνται, 'cramped forces are diffused through the limbs of man' (Empedocles).[90]

He would see there, for example, the taste of food and the odor
and impression of taking in food, and the maker and seller
of food, mixed all in a single complex of obscure dispositions; and in connection with this—if one were dealing with a
clerk*—another complex with paper façades, rows of calculations, tabulation surfaces, money rolls, the feel of money in
fingers, its sound, chair legs, corners of rooms, and so on, and
so forth; and still another with street corners, shop signs, slices
of sky, spots of sunlight, and so on, and so forth. And some
things would be marked by attraction and others by repulsion,
while in the middle would be shadows of men, some without
heads, others without legs (marks of recognition: legs, noses),
some marked by a "yes," others by a "no," and the impression
of a kiss or gnashing of teeth, a hostile glance, and so on—
along with an infernal jumble of names, information, words,
numbers, all of the *topoi* of rhetoric. But through the whole
tangle he would see the pangs of insatiable hunger. Hence the
light of pleasure darts through the pale streak that unites all
things, and the dull radiations that accumulate within it illu-
minate now one thing, now another, so as to delude hunger in
the next instant—without respite. The reality of men is the
shape of a dream, and they talk about it as if narrating a tangle
of dreams, "since the dream comes with a tangle of things and
the voice of stupidity with a tangle of words" (Ecclesiastes 5:2).[91]
The dream is the intimate measure of life, what each person
feels in relation to life such that he is unable to convey its sensations to others. And yet to communicate the tangle of dreams
that is their reality people find conventional words for each
single referent. The man in a dream is naked before god such
as he is: he weighs only what he is worth. All the forms, con-

---

*I say "clerk" because clerks are the souls "implicated" par excellence.

trivances, and words that are not his (but to which he has grown accustomed by convention) fall away. In the intimacy of the dream he is like his forefathers who lived alone and naked. Indeed, when men attempt to render these mysterious dream sensations, they find themselves before the impossible: they "don't find the words" to "express what they are feeling."* But for everyday use everyone says "table," "chair," "square," "sky," "hill," and so on, or "Marco," "Filippo," "Gregorio," and so on.

Οὕτω τοι κατὰ δόξαν ἔφυ τάδε νῦν τε ἔασι,
καὶ μετέπειτ᾽ ἀπὸ τοῦδε τελευτήσουσι
    τραφέντα·
τοῖς δ᾽ ὄνομ᾽ ἄνθρωποι κατέθεντ᾽ ἐπίσημον†
ἑκάστῳ.

Thus, according to opinion, what has existed and
    what exists; all shall grow and die. To each of
    these things men have given a customary name.

Parmenides v. 151[92]

But what do they know about them? They may very well say that they have a mental picture of these things when they shut their eyes and know them through and through, but if they want to say what they are, the image of them dissolves into received bits of information and coordinated data corresponding to diverse sense impressions and to the given thing's use, being reduced—if it means anything at all—to inexplica-

___

*"I don't know how to tell you," "You can't imagine," "You'll never believe," "God only knows," "If you only knew," "ineffable," "impossible to say," "speechless," when something extraordinary ruptures the usual turning of things, and so on.
† Επίσημον = what is according to a conventional sign.

ble sympathy or antipathy, the attraction or repulsion that the given object awakens. It is like when one begins to describe what one claims to see perfectly and ends up scribbling and drawing monograms "because one doesn't know how to draw." Their memory is made up of nodules of dispositions awaiting conventional forms to be recognized; and referring to them with words, people do not communicate or express them but signify them to others in a manner satisfactory for life's everyday uses. Just as a man turns a lever or presses a button of a machine to have certain reactions, which he knows by their manifestations, by the necessities they furnish—though he does not know whence they proceed and he does not know how to create them—so he relates to them only by means of the conventional sign. Thus does the man in society act: he finds the conventional sign on the keyboard prepared like a note on a piano. And conventional signs join together in conventional ways, in made-up complexes. He plays not his own melody but phrases *prescribed* by others.

It is thus that language crystallizes in the aged society. Hegel θωπεύει, 'flatters,' the social man in this respect also, telling him that "as a great man, he makes himself spiritual and is less needful of the little things" (p. 106).* Certainly he no longer needs them and is just like a baby whose loving mother

*Hegel, *Philosophie der Geschichte:* "Es ist ferner ein Faktum, dass mit fortschreitender Zivilisation der Gesellschaft und des Staates diese systematische Ausführung des Verstandes sich abschleift und die Sprache hieran ärmer und ungebildeter wird—ein eigentümliches Phänomen, dass das in sich geistiger werdende, die Vernünftigkeit heraustreibende und bildende Fortschreiten jene verständige Ausführlichkeit und Verständigkeit vernachlässigt, hemmend findet und entbehrlich macht." 'It is an established fact that with the progressive civilization of society and the State, this systematic development of the intelligence crystallized and the language grew poorer and less refined—a singular phenomenon: progress, which grows more spiritual in itself and which promotes and forms rationality, neglects that rational precision and intelligence, finds it an obstacle and can do without it.'

would ensure a life-long means of transportation to avoid exposing him to the *dangers of walking on his own legs*, and not having any need of his legs, he'd have the satisfaction of seeing two limp and shapeless entities in their place.

The trained man is reduced to not allowing his reality to depart from the moment: his direct mode is the sign of a given near-relation. Similar to the dreaming man, who traverses with the light of his point-by-point vision an entire series, because he does not see distant things as if they were near, *he draws himself closer to things in order to see them.* If interest wants to clarify an indistinct element of the present vision, it immediately transports itself toward it and makes it an object of a subsequent vision. I dream that someone tells me about something; then I dream the thing itself (not as something recounted): the vision of my conversation is lost and replaced by the vision of the thing (*A Thousand and One Nights!*). In dream sequential reality does not exist. A potent dream capacity is that of the artist who sees distant things as near and therefore can give them features that appear in their reciprocal relation as near and far.*

The painter who depicts a road keeps the lines parallel *in his eye and hand* when he makes them converge; and all the trees of the same height when he makes them descend; and all of the same color when he renders them gradually veiled by azure, gray, whitishness, violet, or red, according to whether the air is clear, cloudy, or traversed by rays of light at sunset; and all illuminated in the same way when he gradually diminishes their light, as light and shadow penetrate each other.

---

*Boccacio says it well: "Dante Alighieri son, Minerva oscura / d'intelligenza e d'arte. . . . // L'alta mia fantasia, pronta e sicura." 'I am Dante Alighieri, *dark Minerva* / *of intelligence and art. . . . // Ready* and *confident*, my *noble fantasy.*" [Boccaccio, "Dante alighieri son, Minerva oscura," ll. 1, 2, 5, emphasis added by Michelstaedter.—Translators' note.]

Then comes the simpleton and says, "It looks real." The critic arrives and says, "What close-ups! What backgrounds! What line, what light, what air, what color!"

The simpleton takes up the brush. He goes to see the beginning of the street and the end. He sees that the width is the same, and he honestly depicts the lines of the two sides as parallel. And with the same procedure and the same honest diligence he makes the trees all of equal height, the colors equal, and the shadows.

Another simpleton comes and complains that he does not understand a thing, or if he recognizes the street says, "It must be *that street* but I don't understand a thing"; and the critic says, "The idea is there, but the artist lacks training."

The simpleton has brought his capacity for seeing the entire length of the street foot by foot, "of seeing distant things from up close," and has rendered them little by little in the near way he has seen them. He has repeated material vicinity to create the vicinity of distant things. He has not *communicated* the intimacy, the *very* nature of the object, but *signified* it with the appearances that allow it to be *recognized** by those who have already seen it.

Thus he drags himself by speech across the elementary relations of concepts, and no matter how much he turns, he grasps no more.[†]

And the words, remaining obscure and vague in speech, lose the possibility of that fullness of reference wherein their clarity lies. From living bodies that can attach and determine themselves, attaching and determining from so many places and in so many ways, they become material that, according to

*Compare also the difference between caricature and *pupazzetto,* 'puppetry sketch.'

[†]Compare "The Illusion of Persuasion," sections 1 and 2.

the degree of their strength, can orient themselves in one manner only and, sometimes, remain crystallized in such a union.* From precise individuations they become *partes materiales.* Their conjoined mode, as inadequate as their *knowledge,* is limited, reduced almost exclusively to the elementary relations of time and finality.† In the end, the beautiful living organism of a *revelatory* sentence is reduced to a heavy sequence of colorless propositions, like a chain of convicts, linked together with "whiches," "becauses," "and afters," "and thens," "thats," and so on.

*For example, "minister" crystallized in the political sense to compensate for other uses, from "administering" to the "administrator," which is stripped now of the sense in which a minister is an administrator, or an administrator a minister; but each of the two words suffices at each usage to signify the attendant relation. The atrophying process of words composed of prepositions is clear; they lose the sense of their composition in that the prefix loses its government, and they become linked in less pregnant combinations in common ways: if they are verbs, with direct objects, if substantives, with the genitive case (to assign something, the assignment of something).

The inconstancy of roots in the most commonly used verbs is a characteristic example. In its birth, language indicates diverse syntactic positions either by the addition of new words or by a new word for every new position (just as nature, at its lower levels, unites undifferentiated cells with larger complexes: mineral life). The words of a rationally experienced language, like higher organisms more definitely individuated, are articulated in diverse ways with determinate and changeable elements, remaining essentially unchanged in their root character. It thus becomes clear that the same thing enters into a new relation and the new relation is more profoundly experienced. But also in the case of languages that execute syntactic functions by means of inflection, in verbs which, *by continual use contain more social life, concern for sufficient signification* has gained the upper hand over that which befits superior men, namely, concern for *rational communication,* and the verbs take different forms, transforming the root: Greek: αἱρέω, ἔρχομαι, ἐσθίω, ὁράω, τρέχω, φέρω, λέγω, παίω, πωλέω, ὠνέομαὶ; Latin: *edo, fero, volo, eo, queo, fio, sum;* Italian, French: *andare, aller; essere, être; avere, avoir;* German: *sein;* English: to be, to go.

†"Before doing," "After having done," "in order to do."

The man who lives without persuasion, without ever daring to want it, does not have an end or reason in his power that might escape from that point, unless to repeat itself in the past or future. The relations of finality, necessity, and potentiality superficially experienced become confused among themselves and the modes of direct reality.

Thus, if his *intention* touches on a given relation without his knowing, he cannot communicate it with the clear link of the connected organism but must strive with a multiplicity of words to *signify it*. For example, if he wants to say that it is necessary that another do something before he himself does it, he does not say, "I'll do it when you have done it" but, "I won't do it today or tomorrow or ever; first you have to do it; only after will I." To say, "I'd do it if you did," he has to say, "For my part I'll do it—but you do it first."

Or the reverse case: to say, "*Giurerei*," 'I would swear' (= I can swear), he says, "*Io potrei giurare*," 'I would be able to swear' (= I can be able to swear); or "if you wanted me to, then I would do it" (= if you wanted, if you wanted, I would do it); or he uses "provided that" (which indicates a relation of necessity) to indicate the coincidence of two things (which is signified by "in that").*

"But these are pedantic distinctions. You understood what I wanted to say? Enough then."

It is a question of being satisfied. If one is sufficient to himself in the modes of life offered by society, he can be satisfied by signifying conventional things for his everyday use, in conventional modes, and abandoning himself to repeating

---

*In scientific philosophical jargon the subjunctive sense of *in quanto*, 'provided that,' has been lost completely, such that it is used with *che*, 'that,' and the indicative: "provided that this be" becomes "in that this is."

without understanding what others in such circumstances say, in order to be understood in the same mode as others initiated in the same κοινωνία, 'conventions.' Thus can one have a perfected "style" and "language" and never say anything. But when one wants to walk on one's own legs, one must bleed one's words, for "he is blind, homeless, miserable, following hearsays" (Carlyle, p. 78).[93]

But still, giving the impression of saying two different things, some say, "One must become informed about the levels overcome by the spirit as it spiritualized itself in the history of humanity," and others, "One must read good texts and grammar."

It is useless to stir up such trifles further as long as we have established the following: because linguistic perspective consists entirely in the depth of present vision, the organic life of language that pulsates equally in every word and combination of words dulls and disintegrates—as a function of the individual human life—when man's organized foresight (individual security) is reduced by societal security to a single point, an instant.

### 4. THE MAXIMUM WITH THE MINIMUM (RHETORIC)

$$(yc_1 : xc_1 = 0 : \infty)$$

This man of society who, in contrast to the natural man, is weaker to the degree that he no longer must face any of the dangers the latter had to overcome—that is, precisely as weak as he who is incapable of overcoming even the slightest danger and who has no other activity, no larger sphere of action, because his interests go no further than his own life needs, this nearly inorganic will to live—this man, nevertheless, enjoys, in exchange for his tiny learned task and his submission, the security of all that human ingenuity has accumulated in society, what he would not otherwise obtain except by individual superiority, the potency of *persuasion*. With the work of inferior individuality appear the fruits of *superior* individuality: such is the rhetorical significance of *social optimism*. It tells the individual: "He who carries out his duty toward society has the right to live secure." But who gave you the *right to presume that your duty is that which society tells you it is?* It also says: Ἐλεύ-θερος ἔσται ὅστις ἂν καὶ ἐν θυμῷ ἀληθῶς τοιοῦτος ᾖ οἷος μετ᾽ ἀνθρώπων—Ὁ ἀνὴρ δὲ λέγει· Ἐλεύθερος ἔσται—ὅστις ἂν οὕτως ἀληθινὸς ᾖ ἐν θυμῷ ὥστε καὶ μετ᾽ ἀνθρώπων μὴ ἀλλοιοῦσθαι. Ἡ γὰρ ῥητορικὴ πρὸς τοὺς ἄλλους ἀληθεύ-ουσα—Τοῖς ἄλλοις πείθεται—ἡ δὲ πρὸς ἑαυτὸν ἀλήθεια καὶ τοὺς ἄλλους πείθει, 'He who is the same in his heart as he is with men shall be free. But man says: he who is true in his heart to the point of not changing with regard to others shall be free. For rhetoric is true with regard to others in that it obeys others; but truth in oneself persuades others.'

Systematically organized rhetoric, however, nourished by centuries of constant effort, flourishes in the sunlight, brings forth fruit, and profits its faithful. And it shall bring forth still more in the future. And we shall see every man caring for his life alone and thereby denying τὸ ἑαυτοῦ μέρος, 'for his part,' the life of every other, obtaining from others all he wants and living secure before them as if nothing but love of others guided him; absorbed by current affairs and yet dominating others and comprehending things as can the one who is great at the price of his bloodstained justice. Νεῖκος, 'strife,' will have taken the shape of φιλία, 'friendship,' when everyone, socially trained, in wanting for himself, shall want for society, because his negation of others will be an affirmation of societal life. Thus shall every act of a man be rhetoric in action, giving him what he needs without his understanding how.

*Money,* the actual means of communicating the societal violence by which each is the master of the work of others—the "concentration of labor," the "representative of law," the drive belt turning the machine's wheels—it shall be like a divinity raised up to heaven, becoming perfectly nominal, an *abstraction,* when the wheels are so well adjusted that the wheels of each shall enter into the wheels of the other without the need of transmission.

*Language* shall attain the limit of absolute persuasiveness, what the prophet attains by miracle. It shall arrive at silence when each act has its absolute efficiency. And if one of these poor remnants of humanity should one sunny day sense a spark of life, almost a reminiscence across the ages in his sluggish brain, and tarry in thought over the handle of his machine, and distance himself from his labor, his companion will have little difficulty in making him see reason: "Come," he'll say. "It's your moral duty!" The other will understand at once, "It is bread," and he will go to his labor with a bowed head. Καλλωπίσματα ὄρφνης! 'Ornaments of the darkness!' Before gaining the reign of silence each word shall be a καλλώπισμα ὄρφνης, 'ornament of the darkness': an absolute appearance, the immediate efficacy of a word that no longer has but the most minimal, obscure instinct of life. All words shall be technical terms when the obscurity is veiled in the same way for everyone, and everyone shall be equally domesticated. Words shall refer to relations in the same determinate manner for all. As today one says "force of attraction," which means nothing but the complex of effects that surrounds everyone, for which one must assume a sufficient cause, in the same way one shall say: virtue, morals, duty, religion, people, god, kindness, justice, sentiment, good, evil, useful, useless, and so on, and the given relations of life shall be rigorously understood: τόποι κοινοί, 'commonplaces,' will be as fixed in meaning as those of science. Men shall play one another like as many keyboards. Then will the writer of rhetoric manuals have it easy. For the life of man shall truly have become the divine μεσότης, 'medium,' that from the night of future ages shone forth to Aristotle's societal soul. Men shall speak but οὐδὲν λέξουσιν, 'say nothing.' It is to them that Electra speaks when she tells Chrysothemis,

> πάντα . . . σοι . . .
> κείνης* διδακτά, κοὐδὲν ἐκ σαυτῆς λέγεις.

> everything . . . you . . .
> have learned from her, and you say nothing on
>     your own.[94]

I speak of the future in order to have a limit case, but a large part of the future is in the present. Even now no man is born naked any longer: everyone comes with a coat, rich in all that the centuries have provided to make life easy. And the greatest in number are those who attend to life with the greatest attention. Even now man finds all he needs in an established form and believes that he knows life when he has learned the norms of this form and obtains without danger what he needs.

This form, this straitjacket or rhetorical coat, is woven from all the things of societal life: (1) the professions; (2) commerce; (3) law; (4) morality; (5) convention; (6) science; and (7) history. The consciousness of each man rests in the posses-

---

*Clytemnestra—society.

sion of any degree of such knowledge: each man (1) has learned a skill or procures for himself a title; (2) knows how to earn his livelihood by means of this; (3) knows to what extent he may earn it before others and how to demand support against the outrages of others; (4) knows what kinds of feeling and what manner of respect he should have toward others; (5) knows how he must behave and within what limits act toward them; (6) knows the way, the theory of the environment, with which to prevent or redress troubles, and beyond this, how to consult men who are masters of such theory; (7) possesses a foundation of views and prejudices with regard to the past which, with the dross of what has come to pass, fashions for himself a *persona,* as if he were naked and, by nature, such as his environment had clothed him. He knows the commonplaces needed to dress up a societal *persona,* so that his discourse with regard to this life in this form should have the appearance, required and sanctioned, of foresight adequate to every contingency, foresight that responds to every doubt with the right of citizenship—to the greater glory of timid and sufficient optimism. Καλλωπίσματα ὄρφνης! For they are absorbed by the conventional relations and they speak with the obscure voice of these and console themselves for their life. They ask no more. And they want to continue as they are because they believe themselves to be living *persone: their knowledge of life is sufficient to them.* This is their security and peace, their consciousness and joy. This is their trusting glance toward the future.

But they float on the surface of society like a dry pine needle on the surface of water *by means of the equilibrium of molecular forces.* And a light puff is enough to show how insecure was their foundation, how inadequate their security, in the face of the necessity that they deluded themselves they had overcome. When a man sinks below and touches bottom, the fact seems to him and others δεινός, 'terrible': for he feels unjustly struck down, while others sense the compassion of fear. And together they protest against destiny and curse the force that tore through their secure happiness, as if that man had had the right to be confident, as if, his feet firmly planted, he had conquered his place in the sun with his individual value, having eliminated contingencies from his life, and based "his hope on firm foundation."[95] Because their personal comfort is their reality, the calamity that interrupts it is a transcendent force: the devil. This same impotence also reveals itself at every little blockage of each individual's comfort when each, once having attributed value and absolute security to such comfort, after losing it, fails to understand the justice of the other things that consciously or not were the cause of its blockage, and he becomes *enraged*. The cries and curses of the enraged, the continual groaning of the societal machine—*this is the voice of the people!*

But when the plot of calculated forces is torn asunder and violence breaks into life and social man finds himself naked before the forces of nature and of man and must resist with the consistency of his body and character, then the pitiful image of the absolute weakness of the man who "finds neither words nor deeds" becomes universal and obvious to all.

This is why the constant effort of society aims at tightening the plot to strengthen it by means of communal weakness and make it secure against every eventuality.

## ii. The Assimilatory Organs

But how has nature woven, and how does it continue to weave, such a plot against itself? And how is this maintained and reaffirmed in every son of man who, whether born strong or weak and in need of protection, is born yet ignorant of this artifice?

## 1. HOW SOCIAL ΚΟΛΑΚΕΊΑ, 'ADULATION,' IS CONSTITUTED

If the will of nature to actualize itself in a single point by means of the sequence of individual crystallizations culminates in a man's consciousness, which is vast in time and space and in which an almost infinite variety of things is revived by love, then, even in this form, projected outward in time and determined in a certain manner, that same will deprives itself without respite of the actual possession of self and, remaining infinite despite everything, does not attain pure crystal, the absolute individual, *god*. Hence life in every form wants life, and the individual crystallizations attend to their own continuity.

At each degree and with different methods in each case, nature, which is indifferent to the individual, the particular, attends to the continuity of the race and saves it from νεῖκος, 'strife.' Thus even humanity, in whom the final form of will arises, attends to its own continuity. Humanity flees violence by means of society: ἡ φιλοψυχία τὴν κοινωνίαν συνέστησεν, 'The attachment to life has generated society.'

As if by irony, the impulse to this movement of the *principle of weakness* is furnished by the strong. With the menace of foul weather, the uncertainty of nourishment and shelter, and the threat of wild beasts, the first to manage to draw together shelter and food and defense were those who, being the bravest and most resolute, had the least to fear: if they hadn't been such, why would the others have followed them, the others who because of physical weakness and lack of intellectual initiative were without resources, at the mercy of events around them? Initiative always belongs to the strongest, and the "league of the weak" was formed precisely at the expense of the stronger, who, by sheer will to dominate, or by love, have always found a natural sphere of activity for their superabundance of life, to dominate or to love their fellows. But the less they thought of taking advantage of their domination by robbing the others of the conventional signs of power and "the goods" considered as such by men, and the more they wanted the life of others, loving in humanity and presupposing in each the *value* they felt in themselves, that much less were they dazzled by the things to which others attributed *value,* that much less did they adhere to conventional ways, and that much more could they be the initiators of new ways. They did not examine history in order to found their reign, and their reign, if it was not of this earth, was that much more firmly planted in the hearts of men.*

For love they wanted to eliminate *strife* (νεῖκος) among men and offered them a law based on the presupposition that love—the orientation toward the absolute, toward god— exists in all, and the law made them all brothers and united them in mutual respect. In the name of φιλία, 'friendship,' they united and dragged forward vast human currents: the multitudes that followed them, each man with his own mind, *turned* εἰς τὸν βίον, 'toward life,' *that which in the mind of the*

---

*"*Haakon:* What is it that attracts you? The royal crown and the purple robe, the right to sit three steps above all others; what stupidity! If *that* were being *king,* I'd toss the reign into your hat like alms to a beggar. [ . . . ] *Skule:* . . . But this is impossible! This is unheard-of in the history of Norway. *Haakon:* To you it's impossible—for you don't know how to do anything but follow history: for me it's as easy as for a hawk to sail through the clouds. [ . . . ] This thought comes to me from God and never shall I let it go!" Ibsen, *The Pretenders,* Act III, scene 30. [Haakon's final phrase continues: "while I bear St. Olaf's crown on my head." Ibsen 236.—Translators' note.]

*hero proceeded* εἰς τὸ ὄν, 'toward being.' And learning to give their miserable life names that expressed their living sense within that greater life of the prophet, the lawgiver, the revolutionary, they ate and drank and proliferated in the name of Buddha, in the name of Christ.

The bliss promised by the prophet as a secure end—each representing it to himself in the shades of his own desires and freed from the evils by which all are oppressed—they take as a new excuse for their wretched life, the love and torment of their tiny wills. They adapt to new forms, even refusing certain kinds of life as long as they can continue to live and hope, and upon the slaughtered lion minute life swarms with renewed vigor and with the same joys, pains, and pettiness as before. For they find themselves united in his name and by their union stronger and more secure, such that out of his dream of a brotherhood of the good (ἀγαθῶν φιλία) he fostered an organization of hostile wills that make use of his misunderstood symbolic forms—the fruit of his own negation—for the security of whatever affirmation of life they may have (the affirmation of whatever kind of life)—the 'community of the wicked,' the κοινωνία κακῶν.

Although less powerful, these followers act in great numbers and are spurred on by the love of fame or by an ambition which, the more it demands an immediate and easy and nearby satisfaction, the more it descends into lower and lower spheres. And the more needful it is of the society of men, taking this need as a reason for the existence of the society and society's things and needs, the more it—ambition—concedes to the conventional ways of that society: the little reformers, men of state, literary men, historians, journalists, party leaders, demagogues, and those in whose petty initiatives the smallest of frictions come to a head, all those who, encumbered more or less by the baggage of preconceptions, superstitions, the religious and social political knowledge of their time, usurp for their purposes the names of greater men and the forms and words whose effect is already given, and, coaxing others to pursue the needs of the present, "agitate" and initiate or transform or exploit currents of ideas, parties, committees, groups, which all vie—banging together and fighting and entangling themselves—to spur society toward progressive adaptation, the organization of hostile forces.*

And not only do the others believe them *persuaded,* for to the ignorant "being of good faith" is a synonym for "being persuaded," but they themselves—if one excludes the sly—in the *persuasion of wanting to conquer,* taking their need itself as reason, are fooled by their own words. And deluding themselves into thinking that they are spreading their own ideas, they are *unconscious instruments of society:* Λανθάνουσι δου-λωθέντες, 'unknowing slaves.'

But the true organic function of society is science, the workshop of *absolute values,* the purveyor of commonplaces and "special" places. With the "objectivity" that implies the total renunciation of individuality, it takes the value of the senses or statistical data as ultimate values, and with the seal of absolute

---

*A classic example is the *church,* which usurped the symbols and words of Christ to create an earthly *potenza,* 'power.' A modern example is *socialism,* which, maintaining the forms, names, schemes of arguments, and all the phraseology of Marx, has reduced his negation of bourgeois society to an element of reform *in* bourgeois society, aimed at more or less specific and material goals: a reform more or less moderate depending on how much the party leaders needed bourgeois society and, taking advantage of the force given to them by the party, aspired to a place in society. Thus in France socialism has joined the government, in Germany it has created a privileged class more bourgeois than the bourgeois, in Italy . . . about Italy it's merciful to keep quiet.

wisdom it furnishes society with what is useful for its life: machines and theories of all shapes and sizes, out of steel and paper and words.* If it is true that among men of science, who in being such are completely unconscious of the practical end of their study and do not pay attention to it but cultivate science for the sake of science, there are those who have no other

---

*For example, *sociology* (political economy), from its *statistical data of material needs taken as absolute values as if these needs were inherent to the idea of man,* "prefabricates" certain abstractions of life with the aim (conscious or not makes no difference) of making possible the future fabrication of theories of systems, of plans of reform for the progressive adaptation of organized society to the new necessities created by the violence of that which is located or placed outside the organization.

Or *medicine,* which (besides its many other virtues) has created the words "nervousness," "neurosis," "neurasthenia," "neuropathy," and so on, with which it has conceded an almost enviable *persona* to those who in their impotence can do no less than commit furious acts of *rage:* whence their neighbor respects them as *neurotic* and they themselves, all while in the throes of spasms of rage, take pleasure in thinking, "I'm making an impression now—now they'll know I'm neurotic," or they say on occasion, "I'm neurotic, you know," as if boasting of a respectable quality. Thus a comfort is created for the ill that the society has made endemic, and the rage itself is no longer impotent because it can find an end. But the most beautiful service to society has been rendered by *anthropology* (saying nothing of the rest) with its theory of the madness of genius. For among the things to be *explained* by proximate signs and sufficient causes, certainly the most difficult has been the *highest organism:* the one least determined by proximate causes; hence, they resorted to the irrational and said, "Those people are crazy."

He who acts out of motives different from the customary ones, or remains unmoved by those that are customary, is an object of marvel and fear to the others and, like something one doesn't know quite what to make of, because of men's repugnance at allowing the possibility that one from among them might have a motive that transcends their understanding, he is made the object of insulting suspicions. And the phrase "He's mad" is the most common form of vengeance taken by the deluded man against someone whose actions disturb his illusion and force him—terrifying thing—into bewilderment (which proves his own insufficiency). And this has always been the case, so much so that being different from the common norm,

life outside their scientific life, and that they engage in it as something vitally, physiologically necessary to them, having their only hope and joy in their experiments, and risking their lives in order to acquire a piece of scientific information, then it must be said that they are a model of future men because truly is their will completely informed by social necessities and

---

being *abnormal*, means being *crazy* (and even in Greek παράδοξος, 'strange,' was used in a predominantly pejorative sense). It has been this way since the first three men formed a group, for surely one of them from time to time was declared crazy by the other two.

But the service of consecrating a phrase of frightened mediocrity, "That man is mad," by means of absolute scientific authority, which translates it into the dogma, "When 'objective' experience is insufficient to 'make sense' of an individual, that individual is crazy"—this service could not be rendered to society by any other than the most enslaved to it, namely, the modern man of science.

Society cannot defend itself against the truths of those whom it considers revolutionaries or threats to its security by "honestly" responding to argument with rational argument; instead it merely defends itself with violence and the materiality of its own existence. Thus, when unable to imprison them as criminals, it can invoke a condition of insanity and dismiss them. If Christ were to come back today, he would find not the cross but a much worse ordeal in the inert and curious indifference of the entirely bourgeois and sufficient and knowing crowd, and he would have the satisfaction of being a wonderful case for phrenologists and a welcome guest of the asylum.

Surely here, too, Aristotle in a certain manner τοῦ μάλιστα ἐνδόξου στοχάζεται, 'has in mind especially the notorious man,' when he asks in his *Problems* (Section XXX [I:953a10]): Διὰ τί πάντες ὅσοι περιττοὶ γεγόνασιν ἄνδρες ἢ κατὰ φιλοσοφίαν ἢ πολιτικὴν ἢ ποίησιν ἢ τέχνας φαίνονται μελαγχολικοὶ ὄντες, καὶ οἱ μὲν οὕτως ὥστε καὶ λαμβάνεσθαι τοῖς ἀπὸ [μελαίνης] χολῆς ἀρρωστήμασιν, 'For when they become superior men either in philosophy or politics or poetry or art, they all appear inclined to melancholy and in truth are such as to be subject to the infirmities provoked by black bile'; and he cites as examples Hercules, Lysander, Ajax, and Bellerophon; τῶν δὲ ὕστερον, 'and among the most recent,' Empedocles, Plato, and Socrates: καὶ ἑτέρους συχνοὺς τῶν γνωρίμων, 'and numerous other illustrious figures.' Ἔτι δὲ τῶν περὶ τὴν ποίησιν οἱ πλεῖστοι. . . .

in them live the senses of other men and *stomachs preoccupied with the future,* while, with their individuality reduced to sheer mechanism, they carry out the functions of the community ὡς ἰδίαν ἔχοντες γνώμαν, 'as if they had an individual criterion.'

## 2. HOW SOCIAL ΚΟΛΑΚΕΊΑ, 'ADULATION,' IS SPREAD: ΔΥΣΠΑΙΔΑΓΩΓΊΑ, 'CORRUPTING EDUCATION'

μὴ πρότερον μήτε τῶν ἑαυτοῦ μηδενὸς ἐπιμελεῖσθαι πρὶν
ἑαυτοῦ ἐπιμεληθείη ὅπως ὡς βέλτιστος καὶ φρονιμώτατος
ἔσοιτο, μήτε τῶν τῆς πόλεως, πρὶν αὐτῆς τῆς πόλεως, τῶν
τε ἄλλων οὕτω κατὰ τὸν αὐτὸν τρόπον ἐπιμελεῖσθαι.

*to look to himself and seek virtue and wisdom before he looks
to his private interests, and to look to the state before he
looks to the interests of the state and to look to other
matters in the same fashion.*

Apology 36c[96]

Πάντες δ᾽ οὖν ὡς εἰπεῖν ἁπλῶς εἰσι, καθάπερ ἐλέχθη, τοιοῦτοι τὴν φύσιν. Δεῖ δὴ λαβεῖν τὴν αἰτίαν πρῶτον ἐπὶ παραδείγματος προχειρισαμένους, 'Of those who dedicate themselves to poetry most . . . all, to speak frankly, are, so to speak, that way by nature. We must search for the cause first of all, for example, in those who are predisposed.' He speaks of *epilepsy,* of ecstasy. He examines the effects of wine that makes men φιλανθρώπους, ἐλεήμονας, ἰταμούς, 'philanthropic, compassionate, daring,' and then ὑβριστὰς, 'violent,' and μανικούς, 'crazed.' He concludes, οἷος γὰρ οὗτος μεθύων νῦν ἐστίν, ἄλλος τις τοιοῦτος φύσει ἐστίν, 'for the state of that man who is intoxicated is that of another by nature.'

Men who want to have much wood do not pull a strong tree like an oak up by the roots but rather carefully preserve what is a source of riches to them. They do not kill it but give it just enough sustenance to prevent it from dying, so that it might produce more wood. One often passes through partial clearings where the earth seems here and there to form groupings of exuberant power. These low-lying groupings are the thick old trunks with their potent roots, but they are distorted, mutilated in all directions by repeated cutting. One might say that they were long since dead if it were not for the fact that around the scar of the last cut these centenarians, who could have lifted their thick trunks up straight and high and stretched out their verdant crown to resist all the winds, vent with pain and difficulty the force that survives every insult in weak little buds. And when the buds have grown and righted themselves toward the sky, again you will see the little man with his hatchet, and he will mutilate the old indefatigable trunk but will not kill, so that it should send out new buds and continue to give him wood to burn. For he would not be pleased that the tree should grow tall and strong, θαῦμα ἰδέσθαι, 'a miracle to behold,' according to its nature, but instead reduces it to a wood factory because it is what he finds useful.*

Likewise, the little man would not be pleased if his fellow being should grow strong and healthy and secure according to his nature, but with the weapon of society mutilates him,

---

*The mulberry is a beautiful tree, tall and straight, but in the hands of man mulberry trees are poor, mutilated dwarfs. Each year, just as they have put out new buds with tireless hope, they are naked and black, a winter shudder in the midst of the spring countryside, because the silkworms are hungry, and man cares dearly for his makers of silk—until they have made the silk. Then he kills these, too, in order to have the cocoons intact.

molding him such that he should produce things that are useful to its body.*

The worst violence is exercised on children under the guise of affection and civil education. For with the promise of rewards and the threat of punishments that exploit their weakness, and with the caresses and fears that foster such weakness, far from the free life of the body, they adhere to the forms necessary to a polite family, those which, being hostile to their nature, *must* be forced on them by violence or corruption. Still more, faith itself, good will itself is exploited to society's advantage. The great expectation of value is gradually flattered by means of the fiction of value in the social *persona*, always displayed before him as that which he should cultivate in himself by imitation. "You'll be a good boy like the ones you see there going to school, you'll be like a *grown-up*." The myth of this good, studious *grown-up* is created for him, and everything that pertains to study and school acquires a sweet flavor: going to school, the book bag, and so on. And the hierarchy of values associated with the superiority of each class is formed for him: "If you're good, next year you won't write on the blackboard anymore but in a *notebook!* And with ink!" Everyone takes advantage of this temporary *anima*, 'spirit,' 'soul,' which dreams of "*when it will be a grown-up*," in order to violate it, "straitjacket" it, shackle it, direct it to its place among the others, where it will breathe its air on the great dusty path of civilization.

*The service that man analogously renders to calves, lambs, chickens, colts, in order to make them better working machines or better producers of meat, is clear to everyone. That society's dishonest education does the same to young men is immediately apparent to any eye, I believe. It is for this reason that women of our time are poor, miserable beggars in comparison with the women of other times. This is also why the former do everything possible to become "*neutre*," 'neuter.'

From the very first duty allotted to him, all effort tends to render him indifferent to what he does, so that he should perform it according to the rules with complete objectivity. "On one hand duty, on the other pleasure." "If you study well, I'll give you a candy. Otherwise I won't let you play." And the child is forced to put the given signs of script into his head, and the given historical information, in order to have the prize of a candy for his body.

"You studied—now you can go play!"

*And the child grows accustomed to considering study a labor necessary in order to live content, even if, in itself, it is completely unrelated to his life, to candies and playing* and so on. Thus the determinate words, commonplaces, and judgments are imposed on him, all the καλλωπίσματα of convenience and science, which for him will always be devoid of significance in themselves, having only this constant meaning: it is necessary in order to have candy and be able to play in peace—sufficiency and calculation.

When for candy and playing one substitutes profit, "the possibility of living," that is, "a career," being "successful," the "professions," then study or an occupation will conserve the sense of the first duty imposed: indifferent, obscure, but necessary in order that one be able to play afterward, that is, to be able to live how one wants, to eat, drink, sleep, and proliferate. Thus can we create a worthy, irresponsible hand of society: *a judge,* who judges with impassibility, tracing out the projection of the shape presented to him by the inquest without asking himself whether it is just or not; *a teacher,* who keeps eighty or ninety students closed up in a big room for four hours, making them sit still and repeat what he says and study the given things, praising them if they study and are well-behaved, punishing them if they do not study and do not adapt themselves to discipline—and it does not occur to him that he is a man committing violence against his fellows, who will carry the consequences of it with them for their whole life, without understanding what they are doing or why—simply in accord with the imposed program; *an executioner,* who kills a man without thinking that he, a man, is killing a fellow man, without knowing why he kills him. His goal is not to see anything but the indifferent, unquestioned function that gives him the means to live, to be an unconscious instrument.

In this manner, if they make of him a man of science, they make *objectivity* possible. Indeed, he will be accustomed from the cradle onward to think that study is one thing and play another. Thus will he be able to place himself in a position to solve philosophical problems by manipulating concepts taught by scientific norms according to the norms of science, without ever asking their value:

"Theory is one thing, practice another."

"You must make a study of Plato or the Gospel," they will tell him. "That's how you make a name for yourself. But be careful not to act in the manner of the Gospel. You must be objective, observe whence Christ took those words or whether Christ said them *omnino,* 'at all,' or whether they were taken by the Evangelists from the Arabs or the Jews or the Eskimos, who knows. . . . Of course, they are *words* that had a certain meaning in their time. Now science knows how things are, and you shouldn't worry yourself about them. When you've put your book about the Gospel together, *then you can go out and play.*"

The child was told, "Do as your daddy says, he knows better than you, and don't ask '*why*'; obey and don't reason; when you're big you'll understand." Thus also do they encour-

age the young man to pursue his scientific study without asking what meaning it has by telling him, "You are helping to
build the immortal edifice of the *future* harmony of the sciences, and a little of the praise will be yours, too, if men, when
they're older, one day *understand*." But I fear that men are so
well accustomed to this path that they will never be visited by
the whim of leaving their tranquil and serene minor age.

# Notes

1. Sophocles, *Electra* ll. 617–18.

2. The thesis, "*sorba*" or crabapple, into which Michelstaedter has bitten is, of course, rhetoric itself. Its remedy, so to speak, is his spitting it out.

3. Presumably he means Stoicism, Cynicism, Skepticism, and Epicurianism.

4. This is an allusion to the *Triumphs* of Petrarch. See below.

5. Mullach 32–35. This was the edition used by Michelstaedter and cited throughout his study. We have followed each of Michelstaedter's Mullach references with the corresponding passage where available in Diels, citing the fragment and line numbers. Here the reference is to Empedocles, 115:9–12. All Diels references are from part B (the fragments) unless noted otherwise.

6. Michelstaedter's appositive, ὄφρα ἂν μένῃ αὐτόν, is translated in his preceding phrase, "*fintanto che lo aspetti*" or "insofar as [a future point] awaits it."

7. This is an allusion to Petrarch, who, in "The Ascent of Mount Ventoux," quotes Augustine's *Confessions* (X.8.15) in the following manner: "And men go to admire the high mountains, the vast floods of the sea, the huge streams of the rivers, the circumference of the ocean, and the revolutions of the stars—and desert themselves." The passage may be found in Cassirer and Kristeller 44.

8. Ecclesiastes 1:8.

9. Petrarch, "The Triumph of Eternity" ll. 67–69.

10. Ecclesiastes 1:8.

11. Luke 6:39.

12. Plato, *Gorgias* 523a–524a. Michelstaedter has translated the Greek in his previous phrase.

13. Matthew 16:25. Michelstaedter employs ψυχή in the meaning of both animal and spiritual life.

14. Parmenides; Mullach 48–51; Diels 6:6–9.

15. Heraclitus; Diels 91.

16. Empedocles; Mullach 117; Diels 15.

17. Lucretius 76.

18. Heraclitus; Mullach 87; cf. Diels 67.

19. Michelstaedter uses *il dio*, 'the god,' in lowercase with the preceding definite article, in his translations from Ecclesiastes.

20. Ecclesiastes 3:1, 10, 11.

21. Mullach, fragment 60, attributes the words to Heraclitus via Sextus Empiricus. They are not attested by Diels.

22. The Italian *preterita* is the third-person singular of the present indicative of *preterire*, a verb meaning 'to render vain and useless as that which is past.' Michelstaedter is playing on several connotations of the word. For instance, the rhetorical figure of preterition (*preterizione*), which means to indicate the silent aspect of a phenomenon in order to point up its actual importance; also, the preterite is the past tense of a verb, so that one possible rendering of the neologism might be 'time pasts its will.'

23. Φιλοψυχία is a Platonic term. Compare *Apology* 37c; *Laws* 944e; and *Gorgias* 512e. Because of its frequency and its centrality to Michelstaedter's text, we have rendered it in transliterated form without italics throughout our translation.

24. Petrarch, "The Triumph of Time" ll. 49–50.

25. Ibid. l. 65.

26. προϋπάρχει, 'what existed before.'

27. Isaiah 7:16.

28. Mullach 87; Diels 67:11.

29. Parmenides; Mullach 94; cf. Diels 8:34.

30. Mullach 75; cf. Diels 26:12–13.

31. Michelstaedter uses the expression "*via via*," which may be literally rendered as 'way, way,' but with several figurative associations, including 'gradually,' 'little by little,' and 'again and again.' The phrase echoes his immediately preceding use of "*per la via*" twice, which we have rendered as 'along the way' and 'around the way,' as well as his subsequent extended use of "*via alla persuasione*," which we have rendered as 'the way to persuasion.'

32. Compare Diels 26:12–14.

33. Aeschylus, *Agamemnon* ll. 179–81.

34. Mullach 75; cf. Diels 26:13–15.

35. Lucretius ll. 157–58.

36. Compare Diels 85:4–5.

37. Campailla notes: "Michelstaedter adapted this maxim to his own myth: on the first page of his personal copy of the *Persuasion* he drew the lamp [by which he had worked in Florence] extinguished because the oil is overflowing. The symbolic significance of the drawing is explained by a reference in Greek to an analagous drawing traced in the margins of the *Indische Sprüche* ('The lamp burns itself out through a lack of oil / I extinguish myself through a superabundance')." *Persuasione* 197.

38. Aeschylus, *Agamemnon* ll. 104–5.

39. Sophocles, *Electra* l. 120.

40. Ibid. ll. 21–22.

41. Campailla takes this statement as Michelstaedter's adaptation and "correction" of Revelation (1:17): for Michelstaedter, "each person, in order to pass through the narrow door of salvation, must take on himself Christ's cross, must *be* Christ." *Persuasione* 199.

42. The Italian phrase on which Michelstaedter plays here—*fare i conti addosso a qualcuno*—is explicit: 'to reckon someone else's accounts.' Its figurative meaning extends beyond finances, connoting butting into someone else's private affairs.

43. Sextus Empiricus was an early third-century A.D. philosopher-historian, medical doctor, and codifier of the Greek school of Skeptical thought, particularly opposed to syllogistic reasoning. His influence on European philosophical thought, especially of the late sixteenth to the late eighteenth century, can be traced to the republication of his *Hypotyposes* in 1562.

44. The reference is to Uncle Toby, a character in Lawrence Stern's *Tristram Shandy* (1759–67). The novel discloses the repetition of desire implied in the choice of physical life. In *Tristram Shandy* narrating a life never gets beyond the day of the storyteller's own birth. In this sense it is a monument to *philopsychia*.

45. The *Poem of Simonides* is listed as I.19 in *Lyra Graeca Selecta*. The text has been preserved in Plato's *Protagoras*, where it is the occasion of a literary contest between Socrates and Protagoras.

46. As in German, the Italian phrase "*avere ragione*," which is usually rendered in English as "to be right," is composed of the verb "to have" and the word "reason" or "right." It would appear that Michelstaedter includes the article "the" in his phrase—*avere la ragione*—partly in order that it should reverberate within his previous and subsequent discussions of "rights" (*diritti*) and "duties" (*doveri*) and also to reinscribe the notion of a "reason for life."

47. Ecclesiastes 7:20.

48. The verb *subire* carries all the connotations of the English 'to suffer,' including 'to undergo,' 'to endure,' 'to submit,' and 'to bear.'

49. We depart from Campailla's decision here, which brackets a third-person plural verb, "they offer" (*offrano*). We think this suggests exactly the opposite sense of the passage: things offer relations to the thinking agent, not vice versa.

50. The passage is reminiscent of Hegel's suggestion, in the *Phenomenology of Spirit*, of a self-consciousness that is ever expanding in the direction of the realization of the Wise Man. Michelstaedter's task would appear to be the union of philosophy and theology in the compassionate heroism of a single extraordinary individual.

51. This is a reference to Luke 7:22.

52. The German poem is Michelstaedter's own composition.

53. Campailla notes an underlined passage in Michelstaedter's copy of *Jésus-Christ selon Saint Jean* (Paris, 1900, p. 35): "Il était lui, le *flambeau allumé* et brillant, et vous avez voulu, pour un peu de temps vous réjouir à sa lumière." *Persuasione* 200.

54. In the first draft of his *Dialogo della salute* (1910), Michelstaedter translates the final word of the Greek passage, ἀργία, not as 'peace' but as 'inertia.' Argia was the name of the woman with whom Michelstaedter was in love at the time of *Persuasion and Rhetoric* and his suicide.

55. John 12:43.

56. The phrase *sentirsi mancare* is normally translated as 'to feel faint'; we have chosen this rendering at the expense of the phrase's nonidiomatic and more literal sense, on which Michelstaedter plays throughout: 'to feel oneself lacking.'

57. Michelstaedter's phrase depends on the similarity of *affermarsi*, 'to affirm oneself,' with *fermarsi*, 'to stop oneself' or 'fix oneself'; thus, *l'uomo s'afferma*, 'man affirms himself,' and *l'uomo si ferma*, 'man stops (himself),' both resonate within Michelstaedter's description of the stable, immutable, and fixed (*fermo*) value that rests beneath the turning of surface particularities.

58. Michelstaedter takes advantage of the common root of *anima*, meaning 'soul' or 'spirit,' and *animosamente*, meaning 'bravely,' 'courageously,' that is, 'with great soul.'

59. Parmenides; Mullach 76; Diels 8:25.

60. Parmenides; Mullach 153; cf. Diels 19:17.

61. Parmenides; Mullach 67; cf. Diels 8:11.

62. "*Superazione*," a learned expression derived from Latin, combines the notions of surpassing, achieving greater value, being more noteworthy than others, and achieving victory over something or someone. Michelstaedter undoubtedly also has in mind the system of academic preferment.

63. In the original manuscript Michelstaedter placed the initials of the words that comprise the two Greek expressions in boldface with the following notation: "Ἰησοῦς χριστὸς Θεοῦ Ὑὸς Σωτήρ (Jesus Christ-of God Son Savior) form ΙΧΘΥΣ ('Fish'). Those of Ἰησοῦς Χριστὸς Θεοῦ Ὑὸς Ἑαυτοῦ Σωτήρ (Jesus Christ of-God Son of Himself Savior) form ΙΧΘΥΕΣ ('Fishes')." Campailla comments: "For the early Christians the fish was the soteriological symbol of Christ. By converting the singular into plural, as he explains in the text ('If they had only made more fish, they would have been truly saved'), Michelstaedter means to suggest that no one can expect salvation from another, not even from Christ; he must obtain it by himself; he himself must be the Fish. Upon this complex symbolism the author invents the autobiographical creature 'Itti,' the Fish son of the sea, in the poem entitled 'The Sons of the Sea' (*I figli del mare*), which relives lyrically the issues of the philosophy of *Persuasion*." *Persuasione* 201–2.

64. Compare item 37 of Chapter V of the *Aphorismen zur Lebensweisheit* (Schopenhauer 209).

65. Michelstaedter's idea is built once again on a pun: in the phrase "*con ugual mente*" (lit., with equal mind) the latter two words may be placed together to form the word "*ugualmente,*" 'equally.'

66. Ecclesiastes 10:15.

67. Parmenides, Mullach 1; Diels 1:1.

68. The story of Orpheus and Eurydice is another of the basic myths to which Michelstaedter attached great personal importance. The comparison is elaborated below.

69. Plato, *Republic* 486a.

70. Heraclitus; Diels 118:4. "Dryness" for Heraclitus corresponds to wisdom.

71. Parmenides; Mullach 54; Diels 7:3.

72. Parmenides; Mullach 67; cf. Diels 8:11.

73. Petrarch, "The Triumph of Time" ll. 49–50.

74. Petrarch, "The Triumph of Eternity" l. 69.

75. Homer, *Iliad* 22.365–66.

76. Parmenides; Mullach 54–56; cf. Diels 7:3–4.

77. Compare Isaiah 6:9–10.

78. The character, and the scene described, are from Victor Hugo's 1866 novel.

79. Literally, *stento* means 'hardship,' 'poverty,' 'privation,' or 'strained circumstances.' The phrase *a stento* can also mean 'barely,' 'hardly,' or 'with difficulty.'

80. As Michelstaedter's previous usage indicates, the word has two distinct senses: (1) that which cannot be said; and (2) dishonest.

81. "*Nella via vissuta della persuasione*": Earlier editors modified the phrase to read *vita vissuta*, which is a set idiom meaning 'real life.' Campailla follows both ms. versions, which contain "via." The result is a simultaneous play on the idiom and restatement of Michelstaedter's previously elaborated concept of the "path (*via*) of persuasion"; hence, a "true way of persuasion."

82. 'Εντελέχεια· an Aristotelian concept meaning the realization of form-giving cause in activity, as distinguished from ἐνέργεια, mere potential.

83. Leopardi, "Palinodia al marchese Gino Capponi" ll. 203–5 (*Tutte le opere* 1:40).

84. This is Michelstaedter's *paranomasia* or organic *annominatio*, a rhetorical figure in which a common root is emphasized. It is "organic" in this case in that he plays on the actual etymology of *arrivare*, 'to succeed, manage; to arrive' in his use of *riva*, 'bank, edge, shore.'

85. Luke 17:31–33. The Greek passage is translated in Michelstaedter's footnote. The story of Lot and his wife is in Genesis 19. Compare Michelstaedter's earlier invocation of the story of Orpheus and Eurydice.

86. Compare Sophocles, *Electra* ll. 339–40, which Michelstaedter has adapted.

87. Pluto was the god of riches. Procustes was a famous bandit who robbed along the road to Athens. He took in travelers under the guise of hospitality. If they were too long for his bed, he cut off their legs. If they were too short, he stretched them to fit.

88. Compare Sophocles, *Electra* ll. 339–40.

89. Empedocles; Mullach 39–41; cf. Diels 2:4–6.

90. Empedocles; Mullach 36; Diels 2:1.

91. The passage is Ecclesiastes 5:3. Compare the King James version: "For a dream cometh through the multitude of business; and a fool's voice is known by multitude of words."

92. Parmenides; Mullach 151–53; cf. Diels 19:15–17.

93. The reference is to Thomas Carlyle (1795–1881), *On Heroes, Hero-Worship, and the Heroic in History*. Michelstaedter refers to p. 78 of the German translation in Reclam's *Universalbibliothek*. The preceding passage, which is found in "Lecture II. The Hero as Prophet. Mahomet: Islam," runs, "We may call him Poet, Prophet, god;—in one way or other, we all feel that the words he utters are as no other man's words. Direct from the Inner Fact of things;—he lives, and has to live, in daily communion with that. Hearsays cannot hide it from him. . . ." (Carlyle 40).

94. Sophocles, *Electra* ll. 343–44.

95. Petrarch, "The Triumph of Time" l. 45.

96. Plato 209.

# Selected Bibliography

Abe, Masao. *Zen and Western Thought.* London: Macmillan, 1985.

Abruzzese, Alberto. *Svevo, Slataper e Michelstaedter: Lo stile e il viaggio.* Venice: Marsilio, 1979.

Alfieri, Vittorio Enzo. "Michelstaedter poeta." *Letterature moderne* 12 (Mar.–June 1962): 133–47.

Altieri, Orietta. *La comunità ebraica di Gorizia: Caratteristiche demografiche, economiche e sociali (1778–1900).* Udine: Del Bianco, 1985.

———. "La famiglia Michelstaedter e l'ebraismo goriziano." In *Dialoghi intorno a Michelstaedter,* ed. Sergio Campailla. Gorizia: Biblioteca Isontina, 1988. 35–41.

Anceschi, Luciano, and S. Antonielli, eds. *Lirica del Novecento.* Florence: Vallecchi, 1961.

Arangio Ruiz, Vladimiro. "Per Carlo Michelstaedter." *Il Convegno* 3 (1922): 343–62.

Arata, C. *La filosofia della Mitteleuropa.* Atti del IX Convegno culturale Mitteleuropeo (Gorizia 1974). Gorizia: Istituto per gli incontri culturali mitteleuropei, 1981.

Arbo, Alessandro. *Musica e persuasione in Carlo Michelstaedter.* Tavagnacco: Arti grafiche friulane, 1995.

———. *Carlo Michelstaedter.* Pordenone: Studio Tesi, 1997.

Baumbach, Rudolf. *Zlatorog: Eine Alpensage.* Leipzig: Verlag von A. G. Liebeskind, 1892.

Benco, Silvio. "Il suicidio filosofico." *Il piccolo della sera,* 10 Aug. 1913, 1–2.

———. *Scritti di critica letteraria e figurativa.* Trieste: Lint, 1977.

Benevento, Aurelio. "Le poesie di Carlo Michelstaedter." *Critica letteraria* 17.65 (1989): 697–710.

————. "*L'Epistolario* di Michelstaedter." *Esperienze letterarie* 15.4 (Oct.–Dec. 1990): 73–88.

————. "La Persuasione e la Rettorica di Michelstaedter e la 'concretezza artistica.'" *Otto/Novecento* 15.1 (Jan.–Feb. 1991): 119–28.

Benussi, Cristina. "Politica e ideologia in Carlo Michelstaedter." *La Battana* 43 (June 1977): 123–31.

————. *Negazione e integrazione nella dialettica di Carlo Michelstaedter.* Rome: Edizioni dell'Ateneo e Bizzarri, 1980.

Bergamaschi, Giuliano. *Linguaggio Persuasione Verità.* Padua: Cedam, 1984.

————. "Il rifiuto della speranza religiosa e del progetto scientifico in Carlo Michelstaedter." In *Progetto scientifico e speranza religiosa,* ed. G. Santinello. Padua: Libreria Gregoriana, 1985.

————. "Dell'animo come Kairos: Aspetti del problema del tempo nell'Epistolario di Michelstaedter." In *Dialoghi intorno a Michelstaedter,* ed. Sergio Campailla. Gorizia: Biblioteca Isontina, 1988. 97–119.

Bernardi Guardi, Mario. "Bibliografia Michelstaedteriana." *Annali di disciplina filosofica dell'Università di Bologna* (1988–89): 5–19.

————. "La solitaria inquietante rivolta di Carlo Michelstaedter." *Secolo d'Italia,* 27 Oct. 1990, 8.

Bernardini, Paolo. "Il tempo e le tenebre: Saggio su Carlo Michelstaedter." *L'Erbaspada* 1.1 (1984): 21–51.

Biasin, Gian Paolo. *Literary Diseases.* Austin: University of Texas Press, 1975.

Bini, Daniela. "Michelstaedter tra persuasione e rettorica." *Italica* 4 (winter 1986): 346–60.

————. "Carlo Michelstaedter: The Tragedy of Thought." *Differentia: Review of Italian Thought* 2 (spring 1988): 185–94.

————. "Leopardi e Michelstaedter tra autenticità e inautenticità." *Italiana* (1988): 219–27.

————. "Il peso e il pendolo: The Precarious Balance Between Life and Thought." *Romance Languages Annual* 1 (1989): 87–93.

————. "Michelstaedter, Pirandello and Folly." *Italian Culture* 8 (1990): 363–76.

————. *Carlo Michelstaedter and the Failure of Language.* Gainesville: University Press of Florida, 1992.

Bo, Carlo. *L'eredità di Leopardi e altri saggi.* Florence: Vallecchi, 1964.

Boccaccio, Giovanni. *Rime: Caccia di Diana.* Ed. Vittore Branca. Padua: Liviana Editrice, 1958.

Borgese, Giuseppe Antonio. *Rubè.* 1921; reprint, Milan: Mondadori, 1994.

Bozzi, Carlo Luigi. "Carlo Michelstaedter studente ginnasiale." *Studi goriziani* 40 (1966): 3–13.

Brianese, Giorgio. "Essere per il nulla: Note su Michelstaedter e Heidegger."
    *Studi goriziani* 59 (Jan.–June 1984): 7–44.
———. *L'arco e il destino: Interpretazione di Carlo Michelstaedter.* Abano
    Terme: Francisci, 1985.
———. "Il silenzio e i richiami: Per una rilettura de 'I figli del mare' di Carlo
    Michelstaedter." *Studi goriziani* 65 (Jan.–June 1987): 7–22.
———. "Michelstaedter e la Retorica." In *Dialoghi intorno a Michelstaedter,*
    ed. Sergio Campailla. Gorizia: Biblioteca Isontina, 1988. 121–35.
———. "Michelstaedter e i Greci: Appunti per un confronto." *Studi goriziani*
    72 (July–Dec. 1990): 23–48.
Buscaroli, Silvano. "Sacralità ed essere del linguaggio e del silenzio, tra Hei-
    degger e Michelstaedter." In *Sull'Essere del linguaggio e dell'analogia: oltre
    le metafisiche.* Bologna: Tipografia Negri, 1984. 13–34.
Camerino, Giuseppe Antonio. *La persuasione e i simboli: Michelstaedter e
    Slataper.* Milan: Istituto Propaganda Libraria, 1993.
Campailla, Sergio. *Pensiero e poesia di Carlo Michelstaedter.* Bologna: Pàtron,
    1973.
———. "Poesie inedite di Carlo Michaelstaedter." *Rassegna della letteratura
    italiana* 77 (1973): 338–48.
———. "Postille leopardiane di Michelstaedter." *Studi e problemi di critica
    testuale* 7 (Oct. 1973): 242–52.
———. "Un appunto giovanile di Carlo Michelstaedter su Vico." *Bollettino
    del Centro di Studi Vichiani* 3 (1973): 199–200.
———. *A ferri corti con la vita.* Gorizia: Arti grafiche Campestrini, 1974.
———. "Michelstaedter lettore di Ibsen." *Lettere italiane* 26 (Jan.–Mar. 1974):
    46–63.
———. *L'Agnizione tragica: Studi sulla cultura di Slataper.* Bologna: Pàtron,
    1976.
———. *Quaderno bibliografico.* Genoa: Università degli studi, 1976.
———. *Scrittori giuliani.* Bologna: Pàtron, 1980.
———. "Psicologia del comico nei disegni di Michelstaedter." *La pittura nella
    Mitteleuropa.* Atti del X Convegno (Gorizia, September 27–30, 1975). Go-
    rizia: Istituto per gli incontri culturali Mitteleuropei, 1981. 25–34.
———. "Ebraismo e letteratura." *Ebrei e Mitteleuropa.* Brescia: Shakespeare
    & Co., 1984. 24–35.
———. "Le prime interpretazioni di Michelstaedter (1910–1916)." *Cultura e
    scuola* 29.114 (Apr.–June 1990): 17–26.
———. ed. *La persuasione e la rettorica.* By Carlo Michelstaedter. Milan:
    Adelphi, 1982.
———. *Dialoghi intorno a Michelstaedter.* Gorizia: Biblioteca Isontina, 1988.

Carchia, Gianni. "Linguaggio e mistica in Carlo Michelstaedter." *Rivista d'estetica* 9 (1981–83): 126–32.

Cardini, Silva. "Io e cosmo nelle poesie di Carlo Michelstaedter." *Il Ponte* 46.4 (Apr. 1990): 111–21.

Carlyle, Thomas. *On Heroes, Hero-Worship, and the Heroic in History.* Notes and introduction by Michael K. Goldberg; text established by Michael K. Goldberg, Joel J. Brattin, and Mark Engel. Berkeley: University of California Press, 1993.

Cassirer, E., and P. Oscar Kristeller, eds. *The Renaissance Philosophy of Man.* Chicago: University of Chicago Press, 1948.

Cattaneo, Carlo. "La rivolta impossibile." *Aut-Aut* 37 (Jan. 1957): 85–92.

Cecchi, Emilio. "La vita nella morte: Carlo Michelstaedter." *Letteratura italiana del Novecento,* vol. 2. Milan: Mondadori, 1969.

———. "Michelstaedter precursore dell'esistenzialismo." *Letteratura italiana del Novecento,* vol. 2. Milan: Mondadori, 1969.

Cella, Sergio. "Uno studente goriziano a Firenze nei primi del nostro secolo: L'epistolario di Michelstaedter." *L'Arena di Pola,* 29 Oct. 1983.

Ceronetti, Guido. "Il manto delle Ecclesiaste: Dialogo con l'ombra di Michelstaedter." *La Stampa,* 22 Aug. 1984.

Cerruti, Marco. *Carlo Michelstaedter.* 1967; reprint, Milan: Mursia, 1987.

———. "'Leggere' nel Novecento." *Otto/Novecento* 21.1 (Jan.–Apr. 2001): 168–81.

Chiavacci, Gaetano. "Il pensiero di Carlo Michelstaedter." *Giornale critico della filosofia italiana* 5 (1924): 1–2.

———. "Carlo Michelstaedter e il problema della persuasione." *Il Leonardo* 16 (June–Aug. 1947): 129–46.

Cioran, Emile. *A Short History of Decay.* New York: Viking, 1975.

———. *The Trouble with Being Born.* New York: Viking, 1976.

Coda, Elena. "Between Borders: The Writing of Illness in Trieste." Ph.D. diss., University of California, Los Angeles, 1998.

Corsinovi, Graziella. *Pirandello e l'Espressionismo: Analogie culturali e anticipazioni espressive nella prima narrativa.* Genoa: Tilgher, 1979.

Creagh, Patrick. Introduction to *Moral Tales,* by Giacomo Leopardi. Trans. Patrick Creagh. Manchester U.K.: Carcanet New Press, 1983.

De Benedetti, Giacomo. *Il romanzo del Novecento.* Milan: Garzanti, 1971.

Diels, Hermann. *Die Fragmente der Vorsokratiker.* Griechisch und Deutsch von Hermann Diels, Sechste verbesserte Auflage herausgegeben von Walther Kranz. Erster Band. Berlin: Weidmannsche Verlagsbuchhandlung, 1951.

Durkheim, Emile. *Suicide: A Study in Sociology.* Trans. J. A. Spaulding and G. Simpson. New York: Free, 1951.

Ferranti, Franco. *Il peso al gancio: Vita e morte di C. Michelstaedter*. Trieste: Edizioni Italo Svevo, 1983.

Fortunato, Marco. "Michelstaedter tra filosofia e poesia: La nostalgia del fondamento." *Testo* 20 (July–Dec. 1990): 102–12.

————. *Aporie della decisione: Separatezza del soggetto e saggismo filosofico da Weininger e Michelstaedter a Adorno*. Milan: Guerini scientifica, 1996.

Franchi, Gian Andrea. "Carlo Michelstaedter o della razionalità del dolore." In *Il dialogo della salute*, by Carlo Michelstaedter. Ed. G. Franchi. Bologna: Agalev, 1988.

Fratta, Francesco. *Il dovere dell'essere: Critica della metafisica e istanza etica in Carlo Michelstaedter*. Milan: Unicopli, 1986.

Furlan, Laura. *Carlo Michelstaedter: L'essere straniero di un intellettuale moderno*. Trieste: Lint, 1999.

Gallarotti, Antonella. *Il Fondo Michelstaedter della Biblioteca civica*. Gorizia: Università della terza età, 1990.

————. *L'immagine irragiungibile: Dipinti e disegni di Carlo Michelstaedter*. Montefalcone: Edizioni della Laguna, 1992.

Gentile, Giovanni. "Review of *La persuasione e la rettorica* (Vallecchi)." *La Critica* 20.4 (1922): 332–36.

Gentili, Carlo. "La nozione di 'sapere' nel pensiero di Carlo Michelstaedter." In *Studi in onore di Luciano Anceschi*, ed. Lino Rossi and Ennio Scolari. Modena: Mucchi, 1982. 175–86.

Giovannetti, Paolo. "Appunti sulla metrica delle *Poesie* di Carlo Michelstaedter." *Studi goriziani* 77 (1993): 37–64.

Goffis, Cesare Federico. "Gli ultimi sviluppi della critica su Carlo Michelstaedter." *Studi goriziani* 45 (1977): 101–11.

Grene, D., and R. Lattimore, eds. *The Complete Greek Tragedies*. 4 vols. University of Chicago Press, 1953.

Harrison, Thomas. "Carlo Michelstaedter and the Metaphysics of Will." *MLN* 106.5 (1991): 1012–29.

————. *1910: The Emancipation of Dissonance*. Berkeley: University of California Press, 1996.

Hegel, Georg Wilhelm Friedrich. *Phenomenology of Spirit*. Oxford: Clarendon, 1997.

Heidegger, Martin. *Being and Time: A Translation of* Sein und Zeit. Albany: State University of New York Press, 1996.

Ibsen, Henrik. *The Pretenders*. Trans. William Archer. *The Collected Works*, vol. 2. New York: Charles Scribner's Sons, 1906.

————. *The Complete Major Prose Plays*. New York: Farrar, Straus, and Giroux, 1965.

Janik, Allan, and Stephen Toulmin. *Wittgenstein's Vienna.* New York: Simon and Schuster, 1973.

Kojève, Alexandre. *Introduction to the Reading of Hegel: Lectures on the Phenomenology of Spirit.* Trans. James H. Nichols, Jr. Ithaca: Cornell University Press, 1980.

La Rocca, Claudio. *Nichilismo e retorica: Il pensiero di Carlo Michelstaedter.* Pisa: ETS, 1983.

————. "Esistenzialismo e nichilismo: Luporini e Michelstaedter." *Belfagor* 54.5 (Sept. 1999): 521–38.

Leopardi, Giacomo. *Tutte le opere.* 5 vols. Milan: Mondadori, 1973.

Lonardi, Gilberto. "Mito e accecamento in Michelstaedter." *Lettere italiane* 19 (1967): 291–317.

Lucretius, Carus Titus. *On the Nature of Things.* In A. J. Munro, trans., *Lucretius, Epictetus, Marcus Aurelius.* Chicago: Encyclopaedia Britannica, 1952.

Luperini, Romano. "La coscienza di Michelstaedter." In *Letteratura e ideologia del primo Novecento Italiano: Saggi e note sulla Voce e sui Vociani.* Pisa: Pacini, 1973.

————. *Il Novecento,* vol. 1. Turin: Loescher, 1981.

Magris, Claudio. *L'anello di Clarisse: Grande stile e nichilismo nella letteratura moderna.* Turin: Einaudi, 1984.

————. "Things Near and Far: Nietzsche and the Great Triestine Generation." *Stanford Italian Review* 6.1–2 (1986): 293–99.

————. *Un altro mare.* Milan: Garzanti, 1991.

Magris, Claudio, and Angelo Ara. *Trieste: Un'identità di frontiera.* Turin: Einaudi, 1982.

Magris, Claudio, and Emanuele Severino. "Il caso Michelstaedter tra pensiero e poesia." *Corriere della Sera,* 16 May 1982, 15.

Maier, Bruno. "La letteratura triestina del Novecento." In *Scrittori triestini del Novecento.* Trieste: Lint, 1968. 97–102.

Marin, Biagio. "Ricordo di Carlo Michelstaedter." *Studi goriziani* 32 (1962): 101–8.

Marinetti, F. T. *Teoria e invenzione futurista.* Ed. Luciano De Maria. Milan: Mondadori, 1968.

————. *Let's Murder the Moonshine: Selected Writings.* Ed. R. W. Flint. Trans. R. W. Flint and Arthur R. Coppotelli. Los Angeles: Sun and Moon, 1991.

Mazzotta, Gabriele, ed. *Espressionisti.* Milan: Gabriele Mazzotta, 1984.

Michelstaedter, Carlo. *Scritti.* Ed. Vladimiro Arangio Ruiz. 2 vols. Genoa: Formiggini, 1912–13.

————. *La Persuasione e la Rettorica.* Ed. Emilio Michelstaedter. Florence: Vallecchi, 1922.

————. *Opere*. Ed. Gaetano Chiavacci. Florence: Sansoni, 1958.

————. "La scuola è finita." *Studi Goriziani* 32 (July–Dec. 1962): 103–5.

————. *La persuasione e la rettorica*. Ed. Maria A. Raschini. Milan: Marzorati, 1972.

————. *Opera grafica e pittorica*. Ed. Sergio Campailla. Gorizia: Campestrini, 1975.

————. *Epistolario*. Ed. Sergio Campailla. Milan: Adelphi, 1983.

————. *Poesie*. Ed. Sergio Campailla. Bologna: Pàtron, 1974. Rev. ed. Milan: Adelphi, 1987.

————. *Il dialogo della salute e altri dialoghi*. Ed. Sergio Campailla. Milan: Adelphi, 1988.

Mittner, Ladislao. *Storia della letteratura tedesca III: Dal realismo alla sperimentazione*, vol. 2. Turin: Einaudi, 1971.

Monai, Fulvio. "Nei disegni del pensatore goriziano voci annunciano l'espressionismo." *Il Piccolo*, 3 Oct. 1974, 3.

————. "L'opera grafica di Michelstaedter." *Trieste* 20.100 (Jan. 1976): 22–23.

Moretti Costanzi, Teodorico. "Un esistenzialista ante litteram: Carlo Michelstaedter." In *L'Esistenzialismo*. Rome: Studium, 1943. 159–72.

Mullach, G. A. *Fragmenta philosophorum graecorum*, vol. 1: *Poesos philosphicae caetorumque ante Socratem philosophorum quae supersunt*. Paris: Firmin Didot, 1860.

Mussini, Lucilio G. "Clemente Rebora e Carlo Michelstaedter: Rapporti interpretativi." In *In ricordo di Cesare Angelini*. Ed. Franco Alessio and Angelo Stella. Milan: Il Saggiatore, 1979. 320–47.

Muzzioli, Francesco. *Michelstaedter*. Lecce: Milella, 1987.

Nietzsche, Friedrich. *Philosophy in the Tragic Age of the Greeks*. Trans. Marianne Cowan. Chicago: Regnery, 1962.

————. *Untimely Meditations*. Ed. Daniel Breazeale, trans. R. J. Hollingdale. Cambridge: Cambridge University Press, 1997.

————. *The Birth of Tragedy*. Trans. Douglas Smith. Oxford: Oxford University Press, 2000.

Papini, Giovanni. "Carlo Michelstaedter." In *Ventiquattro Cervelli*. Florence: Vallecchi, 1924. Rpt. of "Un suicidio metafisico." *Il resto del Carlino*, 5 Nov. 1910.

Perli, Antonello. "L'etica e l'estetica: Michelstaedter e D'Annunzio." *Studi Novecenteschi* 26.57 (June 1999): 87–107.

————. "La vita e la forma: Michelstaedter e Pirandello." *Lettore di Provincia* 30.105 (Aug. 1999): 25–37.

Perniola, Mario. "Carlo Michelstaedter: La conquista del presente." *Mondo operaio* 4 (Apr. 1984): 108–9.

————. "Beyond Postmodernism: Michelstaedter, Strong Feeling, the

Present." Trans. Daniela Bini and Renate Holub. *Differentia: Review of Italian Thought* 3–4 (spring–autumn 1989): 39–49.

Petrarch, Francesco. *Tryumphes of Fraunces Petrarcke.* Ed. D. D. Carnicelli, trans. Lord Morley. Cambridge: Harvard University Press, 1971.

Pieri, Piero. *La differenza ebraica: Ebraismo e grecità in Michelstaedter.* Bologna: Cappelli, 1984.

————. *La scienza del tragico: Saggio su Carlo Michelstaedter.* Bologna: Cappelli, 1989.

Piromalli, Antonio. *Carlo Michelstaedter.* Bologna: La Nuova Italia, 1974.

————. "Carlo Michelstaedter testimone della crisi del Novecento." *Ausonia* 30.3–4 (1975): 26–36.

Pistelli, Maurizio. "Appunti su Michelstaedter poeta." *Otto/Novecento* 3–4 (May–June 1983): 139–49.

Plato. *The Dialogues of Plato.* Trans. by Benjamin Jowett. Chicago: Encyclopaedia Britannica, 1952.

Polisena, Lucia. "Il tramonto-aurora di Nietzsche e di Michelstaedter." *Letteratura italiana contemporanea* 7.18 (1986): 289–313.

Portinari, Folco. "Michelstaedter: Deserto con poesia." *La Stampa* 3 Oct. 1987.

Principe, Quirino, ed. *Ebrei e Mitteleuropa.* Brescia: Shakespeare & Co., 1984.

Ramat, Silvio. *Storia della poesia italiana del Novecento.* Milan: Mursia, 1976.

Ranke, Ioachim. "Il pensiero di Michelstaedter: Un contributo allo studio dell'esistenzialismo italiano." *Giornale critico della filosofia italiana* 41.4 (1962): 518–39.

Raschini, Maria A. *Carlo Michelstaedter.* Milan: Marzorati, 1965.

Recalcati, M. "Etica dell'essere e etica del dover-essere in Carlo Michelstaedter." *Nuova Corrente* 35.101 (1988): 21–36.

Riccio di Solbrito, Augusto. "Alberto Michelstaedter." *Studi goriziani* 7 (1929): 125–28.

Salinari, Carlo. *Miti e coscienza del Decadentismo italiano.* Milan: Feltrinelli, 1980.

Savini, Alberto. "Dodici note a Michelstaedter poeta." *Aut-Aut* 26 (Mar. 1955): 150–55.

Schopenhauer, Arthur. *Aphorismen zur Lebensweisheit.* St. Gallen: Verlag Zollikofer, 1945.

————. *The Pessimist's Handbook: A Collection of Popular Essays.* Trans. T. Bailey Saunders. Lincoln: University of Nebraska Press, 1964.

Severino, Emanuele. *La Strada.* Milan: Rizzoli, 1983.

Shikes, Ralph E., and Steven Heller. *The Art of Satire: Painters as Caricaturists and Cartoonists from Delacroix to Picasso.* New York: Pratt Graphic Center and Horizon Press, 1984.

Stara, Arrigo. "L'educazione corruttrice: Due racconti di Saba e Michel-staedter." *Rassegna della Letteratura Italiana* 91.2–3 (May–Dec. 1987): 376–93.

Steiner, George. *Language and Silence.* London: Faber and Faber, 1958.

Tordi, Rosita. "Umberto Saba e Carlo Michelstaedter: Dalle lettere inedite di Saba a Vladimiro Arangio Ruiz." *Letteratura italiana contemporanea* 4.9 (May–Aug. 1983): 285–91.

———. "Volontà come rischio: La poesia della logica di Carlo Michel-staedter." *Galleria* 5–6 (Sept.–Dec. 1985): 227–42.

———. "Michelstaedter-Trakl: Volontà come rischio." *Mondo operaio* 14 (Apr. 1987): 116–19.

Verri, Antonio. *Michelstaedter e il suo tempo.* Ravenna: Longo, 1969.

———. "Michelstaedter oggi." *L'Albero* 38.71–72 (1984): 33–55.

Vogt, Paul. *Expressionism: A German Institution, 1905–1920.* New York: S. R. E. Guggenheim Foundation, 1980.

# Index

Absolute, 61–62, 64–66, 78, 83, 142
Absolute individual, 141
Absolute knowledge. *See* Knowledge
Actuality, xvi, 16, 47*n*. *See also* Presentness
Actualization, 141
*The Adventures of Pinocchio* (Collodi), xxii
Aeschylus, xvii, xviii, xxii, 3, 4, 27, 37
Affirmations: as concession, 52; and demanding, 51; future, 23; of illusory individual, 32, 77; inadequate, 67–68, 77; of *persona*, 46–47; and pleasure, 74; presentness of, 22; and proximity of distant things, 55; self, 21, 25, 71, 95; and vaster consciousness, 33
*Agamemnon* (Aeschylus), 27
Air balloon, analogy of, 62, 78–84
Ajax, 146*n*
*Aletheia*, 8
Alone, 7, 10, 11, 121
Ambition, 143
Animals: and immortal souls, 76; as working machines, 149*n*

Anthropology, 145*n*
*Apology* (Plato), 39*n*, 111*n*, 147
Aquinas, xvii
Aristotle: comparison with Plato, xii–xiii; criticism of, xiii, xv; in historical example, 62–63, 83–84; and insight, xvii; and Logos, xix; and modern science, 85, 146*n*–147*n*; and rhetoric, xii, 61; societal soul of, 138; and theoretical appreciation of human condition, xx
Artists, 76*n*, 131
Assent, 91
Assimilatory organs, 103, 140–152
Athenian tragedians, xiii, xviii

Baraden, Nadia, x
Baumbach, Rudolf, 122*n*
Bee and flower, 32
Beethoven, xvii, xxii, 3, 4
*Being and Time* (Heidegger), xvii, xviii–xix, 36
Being-toward-death, 36
Bellerophon, 146*n*

as opposite of rhetoric, xiv–xv;
potency of, 136; translators' note,
7–8, 12–14, 36–37
Petrarch, xvii, xxii, 3
*Phenomenology of Mind* (Hegel), 86
*Phenomenology of Spirit* (Hegel),
xix–xx, 13
Philopsychia: addicted to, 36; defined, xvii, 12, 20*n*; disguises of,
52, 62; god of, xvii, 12, 20, 25, 26,
34, 97; and inability to live without illusions, 61; and modern science, 97; and organism, 20; and
present, 56–57; and security,
102–103; and value, 64
"Philosopher," xx
Philosophia perennis, xvii, xxiv
Philosophy, 70, 71
*Philosophy in the Tragic Age of the
Greeks* (Nietzsche), xviii
*Philosophy of History* (Hegel), 101
*Pithenon,* xxi, 7
Plato: comparison with Aristotle,
xii–xiii; condemnation of rhetoric by, xii; criticism of, xiii, xv; on
death, 39*n*; historical example
using, 62, 78–84; as lacking in
insight, xvii; melancholy of,
146*n*; mirror simile of, 32*n*; and
rhetoric, 61
Pleasure. *See also* Philopsychia: and
actuality of *persona,* 74; correlative, 24; denigration of, 91; as
guide, 21; and illusory individuality, 23–25; of life, 110; light of, 20;
mortal, 19; and pain, 73–74; presentness of, 22, 56; rhetoric of, 75

Pluto, 119
*Poem* (Parmenides), xiv
Point analogy, 92
Possession of self, 11
Possession of the moment, 41, 43
Potency, 15–16, 47*n*, 136. *See also*
Impotency
Power, 144
Pre-Socratic philosopher-poets,
xiii, xviii–xix, xxi, 3, 4. *See also
specific individual*
Present satisfaction, 110
Presentness, xvi, 9–10, 11, 16, 47*n*,
55, 90. *See also* Actuality
*The Pretenders* (Ibsen), 142
Procustes, 119
Professions, 150–151
Profit, 150
Progress of society, 121
Promissory note of society, 118, 125
Property, 112–113, 116, 117
Provisional lives, 31*n*
Prudence, 73–74
Purpose of dissertation and transla-
tors' note on, 3–4

Quintilian, 61

Rage, 31, 36, 145*n*
Raschini, Maria, xi
Rational will, 110
Reading, xxii
Real estate. *See* Property
Reality, 87
Reform, 143, 144
Remorse, 29
*Republic* (Plato), 62